T0340151

The Cambridge Introduction to
William Wordsworth

William Wordsworth is the most influential of the Romantic poets, and remains widely popular, even though his work is more complex and more engaged with the political, social and religious upheavals of his time than his reputation as a 'nature poet' might suggest. Outlining a series of contexts – biographical, historical and literary – as well as critical approaches to Wordsworth, this *Introduction* offers students ways to understand and enjoy Wordsworth's poetry and his role in the development of Romanticism in Britain. Emma Mason offers a completely up-to-date summary of criticism on Wordsworth from the Romantics to the present, and an annotated guide to further reading. With definitions of technical terms and close readings of individual poems, Wordsworth's experiments with form are fully explained. This concise book is the ideal starting point for studying *Lyrical Ballads, The Prelude* and the major poems, as well as Wordsworth's lesser-known writings.

Emma Mason is Senior Lecturer in English at the University of Warwick.

The Cambridge Introduction to
William Wordsworth

EMMA MASON

CAMBRIDGE
UNIVERSITY PRESS

CAMBRIDGE
UNIVERSITY PRESS

University Printing House, Cambridge CB2 8BS, United Kingdom

One Liberty Plaza, 20th Floor, New York, NY 10006, USA

477 Williamstown Road, Port Melbourne, VIC 3207, Australia

314-321, 3rd Floor, Plot 3, Splendor Forum, Jasola District Centre, New Delhi - 110025, India

79 Anson Road, #06-04/06, Singapore 079906

Cambridge University Press is part of the University of Cambridge.

It furthers the University's mission by disseminating knowledge in the pursuit of
education, learning and research at the highest international levels of excellence.

www.cambridge.org
Information on this title: www.cambridge.org/9780521721479

First published 2010

A catalogue record for this publication is available from the British Library

Library of Congress Cataloging in Publication data
Mason, Emma.
   The Cambridge introduction to William Wordsworth / Emma Mason.
      p.   cm. – (Cambridge introductions to literature)
   Includes bibliographical references and index.
   ISBN 978-0-521-89668-9 – ISBN 978-0-521-72147-9 (pbk.)
   1. Wordsworth, William, 1770–1850 – Criticism and
   interpretation.   I. Title.   II. Series.
   PR5888.M384 2010
   821´.7–dc22
   2010025643

ISBN 978-0-521-89668-9 Hardback
ISBN 978-0-521-72147-9 Paperback

For G. J. A.

Contents

Chapter 4 Works   63

Chapter 5 Critical reception   98

Preface

Wordsworth, wrote Coleridge, 'both deserves to be, and *is*, a happy man – and a happy man, not from natural Temperament', but 'because he is a Philosopher – because he knows the intrinsic value of the Different objects of human Pursuit, and regulates his Wishes in Subordination to the Knowledge – because he feels, and with a *practical* Faith, the Truth'.[1] Coleridge, like the other members of Wordsworth's close family group (his sister Dorothy, brother John, wife Mary and sister-in-law Sara), understood Wordsworth's poetic project in a way modern critics sometimes overlook: eager to brand the poet an apostate, conservative or ego-driven solitary, Wordsworth's practical and emotional commitments to his family, community, natural world, as well as to poetry, are often underplayed. His jokey, flirtatious and good-humoured side is similarly glossed over, while his vulnerability and neuroses pale before a critical focus on his assumed narcissism.

Yet Wordsworth sought to teach people how to feel and think not because he felt confident in his own efforts to do so, but rather because he did not. John Stuart Mill considered his poetic ability in similar terms: 'Compared with the greatest poets, he may be said to be the poet of unpoetical natures, possessed of quiet and contemplative tastes. But unpoetical natures are precisely those which require poetic cultivation'.[2] Far from the self-involved figure conjured by those unwilling to engage with his project, Wordsworth was above all a watcher and a listener of his world. His visions, occasionally apocalyptic and sublime, are more often intimate and tender. They are concerned with starlings, sparrows, skylarks, daisies, butterflies, hedgehogs and glow-worms (often seen alongside Dorothy, who anchors his musings), or with individual human beings caught up in moments of everyday emotion – joy, affection, love, sadness, anxiety and loneliness.

That Wordsworth's ontological vision is concerned with the everyday and domestic is borne out in his early poem, 'The Dog: An Idyllium' (1786). Written for the deceased pet of his landlady, Ann Tyson, the poem enables Wordsworth to claim an intimacy with the dog that elevated them both as 'the happiest pair on earth' (24). His poetic attentiveness to the dog is also suggestive of Wordsworth's investment in an imagination concerned with the emotional meaning of everyday events. As Coleridge argued, Wordsworth's ability to 'give the charm of novelty to things of every day' excites emotions in the reader that feel almost supernatural, but that are instead directed to 'awakening the mind's attention to the lethargy of custom, and directing it to the loveliness and the wonders of the world before us; an inexhaustible treasure, but for which, in consequence of the film of familiarity and selfish solicitude, we have eyes, yet see not, ears that hear not, and hearts that neither feel nor understand'.[3]

Even when immersed in profound contemplation, as we find him at the end of *The Prelude* looking up to the moon from the heights of Snowdon, Wordsworth realizes that the 'greatest things' are built up 'From least suggestions' by those 'ever on the watch, / Willing to work and to be wrought upon. / They need not extraordinary calls' (*P*, XIII.98–101). Certainly Wordsworth never recorded having any 'extraordinary calls' to the vocation of poet, obsessively revising and rewriting his poems and doubting his poetic ability into the last days of his life. He was nonetheless spurred on by a devotion to poetry and its rhythms, pauses, cadences and silences as a path to that state of reflection in which our emotional experiences, joyful and painful, begin to make sense. His prosodic style invites readers to think about how they feel after reading a poem in order that they find meaning, not from computational analysis, but from their own felt reactions synthesized with thoughts. This is what Wordsworth meant when he suggested that poetry 'is the spontaneous overflow of powerful feelings': the poem allows us to experience our current feelings – moral, sexual, domestic, intellectual – by rhythmically situating us in a state of contemplation where we recollect who are we are, think about it, and then, as 'the tranquillity gradually disappears', acknowledge the emotion that we feel in that moment (*PW*, I.149).

Wordsworth's concept of memory, then, facilitates not nostalgic reminiscence, but the formation of a backdrop against which we can consider, and so feel, the intricacies of our present condition and how this might affect our being and that of others. For David Bromwich, one of Wordsworth's most perceptive modern readers, the only hierarchy in Wordsworth's work is between those who can feel and those who cannot: 'to be incapable of a feeling of Poetry', Wordsworth wrote, 'is to be without love of human nature and reverence for God'.[4] This introduction to Wordsworth serves to acquaint readers with the emotional spirit of his writing, and also works to blur preconceptions of him as a 'nature poet', 'radical poet', 'Christian poet' or 'conservative poet' in order to draw out the unsettling and yet animating experience the reader undergoes by engaging with his poetry. The first chapter, indebted as it is to biographies of Wordsworth by Stephen Gill and Juliet Barker, offers an account of his life that is contextualized in relation to the period in Chapter 2. Chapters 3 and 4 explore his poetic theory and poetry; and the book concludes with an overview of his critical reception and some suggestions for further reading.

Acknowledgements

Thanks to everyone with whom I have read and discussed Wordsworth, especially Isobel Armstrong, Grover J. Askins, Jonathan Bate, Geoffrey Hartman, Mark Knight, Rebecca Lemon, Jon Mee, Jason Rudy, Charlotte Scott, Duncan Wu and my students at the University of Warwick. Thanks also to Linda Bree for her insightful comments on the manuscript; and most of all to Jon Roberts and Rhian Williams for helping me to hear, as well as read, Wordsworth's poetry.

Texts

The critical edition of Wordsworth's poetry is the Cornell Wordsworth, which includes an array of information on the genesis of each poem, its sources, revisions and chronology. The Cornell Wordsworth follows a prestigious line of editions of Wordsworth's work, edited by Matthew Arnold, William Knight, Ernest de Selincourt and Helen Darbishire, Duncan Wu, Jonathan Wordsworth and Stephen Gill. Readers are encouraged to remember, however, that Wordsworth was so compulsively concerned with self-revision that it is difficult, not to mention unhelpful, to label certain versions of poems 'authoritative'. The Cornell editions are listed below for reference (all Cornell University Press), but for a more portable reading experience, readers can turn to Jared Curtis' abridged three-volume paperback/ebook *The Poems of William Wordsworth: Collected Reading Texts from the Cornell Wordsworth* (Humanities-Ebooks, 2009); John O. Hayden's two-volume *William Wordsworth: The Poems* (Penguin, 1977; repr. 1990); or Stephen Gill's *William Wordsworth: The Major Works* (Oxford World Classics, 2000; repr. 2008).

The critical edition of Wordsworth's prose is W. J. B. Owen and Jane Worthington's three-volume *The Prose Works of William Wordsworth* (Oxford, 1974), also available as a paperback/ebook (Humanities-Ebooks, 2008); but Hayden's *William Wordsworth: Selected Prose* (Penguin, 1988) contains the highlights. *The Collected Letters of the Wordsworths*, edited by Ernest de Selincourt, and *The Collected Letters of Samuel Taylor Coleridge*, edited by Earl Leslie Griggs, both originally for Clarendon Press, are available as searchable databases (InteLex, 2002): all correspondence is quoted from the InteLex database and individual letters are referenced by date in the endnotes. Poems are, where possible, quoted from Gill's accessible *Major Works* and dated by year of composition rather than publication, unless otherwise stated. Wordsworth's prose is quoted from the Oxford edition of Owen and Worthington's *Prose Works*, abbreviated as *PW*. References to *The Prelude*, abbreviated *P*, are to the 1805 edition, as reprinted in Gill's *Major Works*, unless otherwise stated.

Cornell texts

The Salisbury Plain Poems, ed. Stephen Gill (1975)
Home at Grasmere, ed. Beth Darlington (1977)
The Prelude, 1798–9, ed. Stephen Parrish (1977)
The Ruined Cottage and the Pedlar, ed. James Butler (1979)
Benjamin, the Waggoner, ed. Paul F. Betz (1981)
The Borderers, ed. Robert Osborn (1982)
Poems, in Two Volumes and Other Poems, 1800–1807, ed. Jared Curtis (1983)
An Evening Walk, ed. James Averill (1984)
Descriptive Sketches, ed. Eric Birdsall (1984)
The Fourteen-Book Prelude, ed. W. J. B. Owen (1985)
Peter Bell, ed. John E. Jordan (1985)
The Tuft of Primroses, with Other Late Poems for The Recluse, ed. Joseph S. Kishel (1986)
The White Doe of Rylstone; or, the Fate of the Nortons, ed. Kristine Dugas (1988)
Shorter Poems 1807–1820, ed. Carl H. Ketcham (1989)
The Thirteen-Book Prelude, ed. Mark L. Reed, 2 vols. (1991)
Lyrical Ballads and Other Poems, 1797–1800, ed. James Butler and Karen Green (1992)
Early Poems and Fragments, 1785–1797, ed. Carol Landon and Jared Curtis (1997)
Translations of Chaucer and Virgil, ed. Bruce E. Graver (1998)
Last Poems, 1821–1850, ed. Jared Curtis (1999)
Sonnet Series and Itinerary Poems, 1820–1845, ed. Geoffrey Jackson (2004)
The Excursion, ed. Sally Bushell, James Butler and Michael C. Jaye (2007)
The Cornell Wordsworth, a Supplement: Index, Guide to Manuscripts, Errata, and Additional Materials, ed. Jared Curtis (2007)

Life

A longing for the company of others shaped Wordsworth's life, one he met by forming a number of intense relationships. These relationships unfolded with friends, most notably the poet Samuel Taylor Coleridge; lovers, specifically Annette Vallon and Mary Hutchinson; and siblings, particularly Dorothy and John (he was not so intimate with his other two brothers, Richard and Christopher). Born in the Lake District in 1770, Wordsworth's early life was marked by a dependency on Dorothy, to whom he was especially devoted in the absence of his father, who often worked away from home. He was also close to his mother, a figure whom he recalled as a moral and upright influence, balancing his 'moody and violent' temperament:

> I remember also telling her on one week day that I had been at church, for our school stood in the churchyard, and we had frequent opportunities of seeing what was going on there. The occasion was, a woman doing penance in the church in a white sheet. My mother commended my having been present, expressing a hope that I should remember the circumstance for the rest of my life. 'But', said I, 'Mama, they did not give me a penny, as I had been told they would'. 'Oh', said she, recanting her praises, 'if that was your motive, you were very properly disappointed'. (*PW*, III.371–2)

Wordsworth's cynicism deepened when his mother died of pneumonia in 1778, and Dorothy was sent to live with his mother's cousin, Elizabeth Threlkeld, in Halifax. When their father died just five years later in 1783, Wordsworth, Dorothy and John came to rely on each other, developing an affectionate bond that both inspired and attracted to it figures such as

1

Coleridge, fellow writers Charles Lamb and Thomas De Quincey, and the sisters Mary and Sara Hutchinson, whom Wordsworth had met at primary school in Penrith. Separated from Dorothy and the Hutchinsons at grammar school in Hawkshead, however, Wordsworth sought solace in his new environment. The natural world surrounding Hawkshead, Windermere and Coniston offered Wordsworth the most stunning of mountainous landscapes from which to borrow poetic images and sounds; and he quickly forged strong familial ties with his boarding family, Ann and Hugh Tyson. In addition, his teachers and the books they taught granted Wordsworth new worlds in which to imaginatively escape. Ovid's *Metamorphoses* and Fox's *Book of Martyrs* encouraged his taste for Homer, Virgil, Juvenal and Cicero; and he recalls reading 'all Fielding's works, *Don Quixote*, *Gil Blas*, and any part of Swift that I liked' (*PW*, III.372).

Wordsworth was an unusual student, not for his intellectual brilliance, but because of his eagerness to read widely in all subjects. Thomas Bowman, a former headmaster of Hawkshead, even reported that 'he believed that he did more for William Wordsworth by lending him books than by his teaching … it was books he wanted, all sorts of books; Tours and Travels, which my father was partial to, and Histories and Biographies, which were also favourites with him; and Poetry – that goes without saying'.[1] Wordsworth later admitted that he read little contemporary literature ('God knows my incursions into the fields of modern literature, excepting in our own language three volumes of Tristram Shandy, and two or three papers of the Spectator, half subdued – are absolutely nothing').[2] Yet he was nevertheless very much taken by the then fashionable emotive sensibility promoted by eighteenth-century poets like Helen Maria Williams and Charlotte Smith, as well as by the graveyard poets Edward Young and Thomas Gray.

Deep in his studies, of poetry and the natural world, Wordsworth was shaken by his father's death in 1783, not only because it left him orphaned and dependent on relatives, but also because it reminded him how distant he had been from his father. Worse still was the discovery that the family finances were tangled up in the affairs of the much-hated landowner, Sir James Lowther, whom Wordsworth's father had worked for as a law-agent and investor. Unable to retrieve these investments (the claim was not settled until 1802), the Wordsworth children were left homeless, a state of affairs that only served to increase the intimacy between Wordsworth and Dorothy, and also with their friend, Mary Hutchinson. The poet remembers his early relationships with the two women in *The Prelude* as 'the blessed time of early love' (*P*, XI.318), a period that stood in stark contrast to his imminent life at university, where he was to take his degree and prepare for ordination.

Education and politics

When he was 17, Wordsworth enrolled at St John's, Cambridge, a college with strong connections to Hawkshead and where his uncle, William Cookson, was a Fellow. He was granted a 'sizar's place', which meant that he received financial support in exchange for menial errands, and he added to this scholarship with academic awards, proving himself an initially enthusiastic, confident and committed student. Yet he was soon disillusioned by his lived experience of Cambridge. As he wrote in *The Prelude*, 'I was not for that hour, / Nor for that place' (*P*, III.80–1), one that he found intellectually and imaginatively outdated. Academic achievement, he feared, was based not on hard work at Cambridge, but on 'Honour misplaced, and Dignity astray' (*P*, III.635). For example, when the college Master died shortly after his arrival, Wordsworth, whose poetic aspirations were already apparent, was asked to write an elegy for him. This appalled Wordsworth, who understood elegy as a personal exploration of genuine grief: the expectation that he should show false emotion for the sake of college duty simply reinforced his sense of Cambridge as a dead and alienating place that produced only imprudent ministers and lawyers. His results plummeted and he left with only a basic degree.

For Wordsworth, real education was reflective rather than accumulative. He learned, not by accruing facts and figures, but through his experiences of poetry, nature and travel as shared with his close family and friends. His pedagogy was one wherein the individual spends time thinking about his or her own situations and experiences before searching out new ones. Wordsworth put this into practice in his poem, 'An Evening Walk' (1788–9), addressed to his strongest ally, Dorothy. Yet even Dorothy was not party to the walking tour of Europe Wordsworth planned with his friend Robert Jones for the summer of 1790. Travelling for three months and covering 3,000 miles (2,000 of them on foot), the two men excited what Wordsworth described as a 'general curiosity' both in those they met abroad, and also in those Cambridge acquaintances who had reproved the scheme as 'mad & impracticable'. Their tour was, indeed, extraordinary: on reaching Calais on 13 July, Wordsworth and Jones were immediately thrown into the first anniversary celebrations of the fall of the Bastille, the 'whole nation mad with joy,' Wordsworth wrote, 'in consequence of the revolution'.[3]

Moving from these celebrations to explore the monastery of the Grande Chartreuse, Lake Geneva and the Alps at the Simplon Pass, Wordsworth found his return to England a difficult one. Finishing his studies in 1791, he left the stuffiness of Cambridge for the equally hostile clamour of London, finding respite in a few weeks' stay with Dorothy and also a visit to Jones in Wales, where together they climbed Snowdon. Here was a habitat in which Wordsworth could reflect on his months in London, a period in which he had absorbed the political fervour produced by English reactions to the Revolution in France. Public debate was alive both in the capital's more radical meeting places – dissenting chapels, bookshops and coffee houses – and also in parliament, where Wordsworth attended debates in the Commons. He listened to the conservative Irish politician Edmund Burke speak against the Revolution, and the radical pamphleteer Thomas Paine, feminist philosopher Mary Wollstonecraft and political theologian and scientist Joseph Priestley speak for it. Urged by their dialogue to consider his own position on France, Wordsworth decided to return there, partly to learn French and so improve his career prospects (his brothers were already employed, Richard in the law and John in the East India Company), but also to think more about what the idea of revolution really meant.

Wordsworth's second trip to France, from November 1791 to December 1792, was one of the most important years of his life: emotionally (he experienced his first love affair); politically (he saw firsthand the crushing impact of the Revolution on the poor); and intellectually (he wrote his first significant poetry). In Paris, Wordsworth socialized using a series of letters of introduction from Charlotte Smith, whose self-consciously elegiac and sentimental poetry provided the main model for his own work of this period. He also hoped to meet the poet Helen Maria Williams, but on just missing her during a visit to Orléans, Wordsworth was instead introduced to a French family called the Vallons. He was immediately attracted to their daughter, Marie Anne, known as Annette, and by February 1792, he moved to Blois to spend time with her. While we know little about their love affair at this time, we do know that their child, Anne-Caroline Wordsworth, was baptized on 15 December, a ceremony Wordsworth was unable to attend. By the end of the month, he was back in England, and did not see either Annette or Anne-Caroline for another ten years.

Critics are divided on the reasons for this separation: some suggest that the Vallons' Roman Catholicism, a religion Wordsworth despised, prevented him from committing to the family; some claim that his already-established affection for Mary got in the way; and others suggest that the circumstances of Britain's war with France severed the lovers' connection. These same circumstances also ended Wordsworth's other ardent relationship of this period with a captain in the French Royalist army called Michael Beaupuy. Wordsworth considered Beaupuy a model humanist, philosopher and philanthropist, who guided him through a France that was no longer elated by the Revolution. It was with Beaupuy in Orléans that Wordsworth encountered the 'hunger-bitten Girl' of *The Prelude* (*P*, IX.512), a symbol of the food riots now commonplace across rural France. Concerned by reports of this rioting, Dorothy urged her brother to return home, distressed as she was by 'daily accounts of Insurrections & Broils'.[4] She was right to worry: Wordsworth had returned to France in the aftermath of the imprisonment of the King and the September Massacres, and escaped back to England only a few weeks before Louis XVI was guillotined on 21 January 1793.

Now desperate to earn a living, in part to support his French family, Wordsworth begrudgingly decided he would take up William Cookson's offer of a curacy. On discovering his liaison with Annette, however, his uncle withdrew all forms of assistance. Relieved, Wordsworth finally admitted to himself that he could only really find fulfilment in writing poetry. His early publications, 'An Evening Walk' and 'Descriptive Sketches' (1793), were issued by the radical publisher, Joseph Johnson, and, while not financially successful, they were noticed by those who would prove most important in his formation as a poet: Dorothy and Samuel Taylor Coleridge. Dorothy was in fact rather critical of the volumes, writing that while she believed the 'Poems contain many Passages exquisitely beautiful', they 'also contain many Faults, the chief of which are Obscurity'.[5] It was this propensity for aesthetic judgement, as well as her unwavering emotional support, that Wordsworth most respected, and her comments inspired him to improve his writing.

Wordsworth's particular affection for Dorothy, as for his brother John, was rooted, not only in familial love, but also in their capacity to embody a poetic sensibility he sought to express linguistically. Now lodging with Richard in London, he felt a deep need for the sensitive companionship of his sister, longing for someone to share his frustration at England's refusal to enter into the revolutionary spirit he had encountered in France. The government were quick to suppress dissent at home for fear it would spill over into civil war, and the apparent radicalism of groups such as the London Corresponding Society appeared tame in comparison to the fervour of Beaupuy. When Richard Watson, the Anglican Bishop of Llandaff, echoed Burke's argument that the Revolution had transformed the French into 'an humiliating picture of human nature, when its passions are not regulated by religion or controlled by law', Wordsworth was quick to respond. *A Letter to the Bishop of Llandaff*, written in 1793, asserted the rights of the French to choose their own kind of government, one that would above all defend and support the poor. Terrified his brother would be prosecuted for treason, Richard urged Wordsworth to 'be cautious in writing or expressing your political Opinions', and the pamphlet was not published until after Wordsworth's death.[6]

Wordsworth was otherwise very vocal in expressing his anger at England's failure to embrace radicalism. His family remained so unnerved by his dissenting views that they even tried to separate him from Dorothy for fear of untoward influence. The two therefore met secretly in January 1794 at their friend William Calvert's home in the Lake District. Wordsworth had been touring the country with Calvert, visiting landmarks that would later appear in his poetry: Stonehenge, Salisbury Plain, Tintern Abbey and Goodrich Castle. He might even have briefly returned to France to visit Annette, claiming later in life to have witnessed firsthand the execution of a journalist called Antoine Joseph Gorsas in October 1793. He was back in the Lake District by Christmas, however, again meeting Dorothy at Calvert's, where she began what would become a regular job – entering fair copies of his poems into a home-made notebook. The Calvert family also financially supported Wordsworth, their younger son Raisley leaving him £900 in his will after the poet had nursed him through tuberculosis. With this money, Wordsworth could finally commit to a publishing career, and he immediately acted on a plan to establish a humanist journal with a friend from Cambridge called William Mathews.

The journal was called the *Philanthropist*, and was largely informed by Wordsworth's discovery of the political philosopher William Godwin and his *Enquiry Concerning Political Justice and Its Influence on Morals and Happiness* (1793). Godwin's main argument in the *Enquiry* was that only reason and truth, not violence or revolution, would create change in society. The argument appealed to Wordsworth because it suggested that revolution was motivated on the one hand, by the ideals of fairness and honesty, and on the other, by literature and education. While the *Philanthropist* project stalled, Wordsworth's interest in Godwin intensified and he returned to London in early 1795 to join a circle of radical thinkers, including the poet George Dyer (who had introduced Coleridge to Godwin the previous year) and Godwin himself. Wordsworth also met Basil Montagu at this time, a struggling lawyer and widower with a young son. Montagu found Wordsworth a profoundly supportive presence, so much so that one of his wealthier friends offered the poet and his sister a house in Dorset rent-free on the condition that they would take care of Montagu's son, also called Basil. Wordsworth jumped at the idea, and moved into the house, known as Racedown Lodge, in 1795. He was desperate to leave London, disillusioned with its high society and bored with Godwin's politics, which he now considered excessively empirical. In reaction against the city, the poet made Racedown into a warm and intimate family community, comprising himself, Dorothy, little Basil, Mary Hutchinson and his new friend, Coleridge.

Coleridge

Wordsworth met Coleridge in 1795 and the two men were immediately enamoured with each other. Wordsworth found Coleridge a visionary and intellectually brilliant poet and philosopher, and Coleridge was mesmerized by his new admirer's commitment to exploring new modes of writing and thinking. In July 1797, Wordsworth and Dorothy were invited to Coleridge's house in Nether Stowey, a village in northwest Somerset where he had 'retired' from active political activity to be with his wife, Sara Fricker. The Coleridges were then hosting the essayist and children's writer Charles Lamb, who was desperately in need of respite after his schizophrenic sister, Mary, had murdered their mother. Lamb later recalled how comforted he was by Wordsworth's poem, 'Lines Left upon a Seat in a Yew-tree', recited to the group in an adjoining garden owned by the tanner and book collector, Thomas Poole. Yet it was the strong relationship between Wordsworth and Dorothy that provided the foundations for their community in Somerset. The brother and sister were never again parted after moving into Racedown, and Coleridge was a constant presence wherever they moved, before and after Wordsworth's marriage to Mary Hutchinson in 1802.

Only a week after arriving at Nether Stowey, Wordsworth and Dorothy rented Alfoxden House just four miles away from Coleridge, where they had 'a view of the sea, over a woody meadow-country'.[7] Coleridge frequently stayed overnight at Alfoxden without his wife, and he, Dorothy and Wordsworth were inseparable during 1797 and 1798, forever raving about each other. 'His conversation', Dorothy wrote of Coleridge, 'teems with soul, mind, and spirit. Then he is so benevolent, so good tempered and cheerful, and, like William, interests himself so much about every little trifle.' Coleridge reciprocated: 'She is a woman indeed! – in mind, I mean, & heart … her eye watchful in minutest observation of nature – and her taste a perfect electrometer – it bends, protrudes, and draws in, at subtlest beauties & most recondite faults.' His admiration for her brother, however, was beyond any he had previously felt: 'The Giant Wordsworth – God love him!' he declared, writing that 'his soul seem[s] to inhabit the universe like a palace, and to discover truth by intuition, rather than by deduction'.[8]

Together the three walked miles over the nearby Quantock Hills, often through the night, discussing and writing poetry. As Wordsworth 'mumbl[ed] to hissel' along t'roads', as one local observed, Dorothy followed behind memorizing his words and transcribing them into notebooks.[9] Such behaviour struck the native community as extremely suspicious, however, and a government agent called Daniel Lysons was soon employed by the Home

Office to track their activity. Their communal set-up immediately confused Lysons: 'the master of the House has no wife with him but only a woman who passes for his Sister', he wrote, but he was equally concerned by their knowledge of French politics and literature as by their strange accents (northern, but assumed to be French).[10] He was also concerned with the group's neighbours at Nether Stowey, who included the notorious 'Citizen' John Thelwall, founder of the London Corresponding Society, and feared in Britain as a potential terrorist.

While all of Lysons' accusations were unfounded, the commotion forced the group out of Alfoxden, and Wordsworth, Coleridge and Dorothy grew desperate to leave England. Wordsworth was miserable after his play *The Borderers* (1796–7) was rejected by Covent Garden; and Coleridge was deep in a feud with the poet Robert Southey, with whom he had previously studied and collaborated. Southey was both jealous of Wordsworth, and also upset that Coleridge had tasked Wordsworth, and not him, with the writing of a new Miltonic philosophic epic (which would eventually become *The Prelude*). This *Paradise Lost* (1667) for the nineteenth century was to be entitled *The Recluse or Views of Nature, Man, and Society*, 'addressed to those, who in consequence of the complete failure of the French Revolution have thrown up all hopes of the amelioration of mankind, and are sinking into an almost epicurean selfishness'.[11]

The idea developed partly out of Wordsworth, Dorothy and Coleridge's conception of a new kind of poetry, a hybrid of the lyric and the ballad that would speak to a broad readership on different levels. While still at Alfoxden, Wordsworth and Coleridge had decided to write a collection of these poems together called the *Lyrical Ballads* in order to raise money for a trip to Germany to research *The Recluse*. In reality, Wordsworth wrote most of the poems, but the project was undoubtedly communal, Coleridge's politics and Dorothy's journals appearing fragment-like throughout the collection. Ensuing revisions, however, notably the 1800 and 1802 editions, are dominated by Wordsworth, who added numerous prefaces and appendices that ultimately distanced Coleridge, whose poems were largely excised.

J. & A. Arch published the first edition of the *Lyrical Ballads* in October 1798, their friend Joseph Cottle, to whom the poems were promised, having rejected the volume as a potentially unprofitable investment. By this time, Wordsworth, Dorothy and Coleridge were already in Hamburg. While Coleridge, subsidized by a wealthy benefactor, was eager to travel to the university towns of Ratzeburg and Göttingen, Wordsworth and Dorothy longed for Alfoxden. The two struggled on insufficient savings and felt generally isolated: neither could speak German and Dorothy was almost constantly ill during the trip. Settling in the relatively cheap city of Goslar for the duration of a ferocious

German winter, the siblings had only each other, their personal memories, thoughts and feelings, and a few books for company. Deep in the Gothic poetry of Gottfried Bürger and Thomas Percy's collection of manuscript ballads, *Reliques of Ancient English Poetry* (1765), Wordsworth began to write a series of his own ghostly ballads, including the Lucy and Matthew poems. He also wrote over 400 lines of the poem Coleridge had set him to write, and by April he and Dorothy had found their way to Göttingen to visit their friend and make plans to return to England. Eager to re-establish the community at Racedown in the Lake District, Wordsworth toured the area with Coleridge before renting a house just north of his old school in a village called Grasmere.

Home at Grasmere

With Mary, Wordsworth and Dorothy remained resident in Grasmere for the rest of their lives. After the less than warm reception they had received in Alfoxden and Germany, Grasmere felt like a welcoming paradise, their cottage overgrown with brambles and shrubs, framed by an orchard at the back and overlooking 'the lake, the church, helm cragg [sic], and two thirds of the vale'.[12] In 1800, by which time Coleridge was almost a permanent guest, the Wordsworths' brother John had joined them, staying for much of the year and helping to furnish the cottage and develop the gardens. John was a model of sensitivity, judgement and modesty for Wordsworth, 'his eye for the beauties of Nature [as] fine and delicate as ever Poet or Painter was gifted with; in some discriminations, owing to his education and way of life, far superior to any person's I ever knew'.[13] John promised to financially support his siblings using money earned for his work at the East India Company, and planned to build himself a cottage near to them on his return from his next trip. Energized by the familial support of Dorothy, John and Coleridge, Wordsworth continued to work on *The Recluse*, moving on from the introductory lines he had composed in Germany (referred to by modern critics as *The Two-Part Prelude*) to begin the first book on 'nature': 'Home at Grasmere' (*c*.1800).

Many of the poems Wordsworth wrote during this time focus either on events and people he encountered in the Lakes, or on particular objects he observed around him, a bird or a flower, for example. It was his emotional response to people and the natural world, however, which remained key for Wordsworth, who regularly made himself ill in his compulsion to fine-tune and revise his verse. He felt a great responsibility to his readers, believing that poetry might reproduce the kind of 'domestic affections' and communal love currently being destroyed by industrialization. He was himself dependent on the presence of a loving community of people around him, which, in 1802, included Dorothy, John, Coleridge, Mary and Mary's sister Sara. The group even carved their initials on a stone now known as 'Sara's Rock' during a walk between Grasmere and Keswick as a testimony to this bond.

Relationships within the group flourished. Coleridge fell in love with Sara (even though he was not to separate from his wife until 1806), and Wordsworth was intent on marrying Mary, but first had to settle his affairs with Annette and Anne-Caroline. Now free to travel to France due to the temporary peace established by the Treaty of Amiens (1802), Wordsworth, accompanied by Dorothy, set out for Calais to see the Vallons. Annette gracefully accepted his intention to marry Mary, and when the Wordsworths returned to Britain, they discovered that the Lowther claim that had so haunted the family since their father's death was finally settled, granting Wordsworth some added financial security.

Wordsworth married Mary on 4 October 1802, in the village church of Brompton-by-Sawdon in Yorkshire, near to the Hutchinson farm at Gallow Hill. Critics make much of Dorothy's anxious state prior to her brother's marriage, but the three adults were undoubtedly close, and Dorothy confessed to a friend that she had 'long loved Mary Hutchinson as a Sister'.[14] Perhaps to placate any potential fears his sister might have felt towards his marriage, Wordsworth asked Dorothy to wear Mary's ring the night before the wedding, intimating that he would remain as loyal to her as to his new wife. On the day of the marriage, which Dorothy did not attend, she records in her journal: 'I gave him the wedding ring – with how deep a blessing! I took it from my forefinger where I had worn it the whole of the night before – he slipped it again onto my finger and blessed me fervently.'[15] Any anxiety Dorothy might have felt was dispelled by the reality of events anyway: the ceremony was over soon after 8am, when Wordsworth had returned home to Dorothy to prepare for their move back to Grasmere, where the three embodied, wrote Coleridge, 'the happiest Family, I ever saw'.[16]

Wordsworth's relationship with Coleridge, however, was becoming strained. In the summer of 1803, the poet decided to tour Scotland with him and also Dorothy in an attempt to smooth things over, despite Mary having just given birth to their first child, John, in June. Soon into the six-week tour, Coleridge announced that he was ill and wished to travel alone, even though Wordsworth and Dorothy often ended up staying in cottages and inns only just vacated by their friend. The three felt alienated further by their surroundings, having no grasp of Gaelic and astonished by the extreme poverty apparent in the subsistence economy communities of the north. Wordsworth was once again relieved to return to Grasmere, and more so when he was presented with the title deeds to an estate in the hamlet of Applethwaite near Keswick by a new acquaintance: Sir George Beaumont.

Beaumont was a painter, art patron and collector, and greatly admired the *Lyrical Ballads* after being introduced to the volume by the novelist Walter Scott, whom Wordsworth had met in Scotland. He and his wife Margaret remained steady champions of Wordsworth's poetry, but more importantly, offered him friendship just as his relationship with Coleridge was beginning to break down. Coleridge kept insisting that he was 'SO VERY VERY ill' during this period, but he was in fact addicted to the opium that he took to relieve both his physical complaints and the 'scream-dreams' he claimed haunted his sleep.[17] While Dorothy nursed him for several weeks in Grasmere, Coleridge finally decided to leave the Wordsworths for Sicily and Malta where he could convalesce in a warmer climate.

Coleridge wrote Wordsworth and Dorothy an emotional farewell letter from Portsmouth in April 1804, effusively expressing a love for them both which had been significantly revitalized by his final weeks at Grasmere. Not only had the two men made a pilgrimage to Greenhead Ghyll where, 'sitting on the very Sheepfold dear William read to me his divine Poem, Michael', but Wordsworth had also read him 'his divine Self-biography' to which he was now fully committed.[18] The poem still remained what he described as a 'tributary' or 'portico' to *The Recluse*, but Wordsworth continued to revise and expand this 'prelude' to include not only memories from his life, but extended reflections on ideas such as the imagination, experience, truth and love.[19] The poem had become a meditation on how we shape our existence through an imaginative understanding of our environment enhanced by both our love for others and capacity for 'chearfulness in every act of life' (*P*, XIII.117). Such cheeriness, Wordsworth reminds the reader throughout *The Prelude*, is dependent on its opposite emotion – grief – and it was while reflecting on this that he was to experience the deepest sorrow of his adult life.

Friendship and love

On 5 February 1805, John Wordsworth's ship, the *Earl of Abergavenny*, sank just off Portland Bill, killing around 250 passengers and crew. As captain, Wordsworth's brother remained at his command throughout the night, but was swept out to sea just after midnight. While Richard immediately wrote to Wordsworth and Dorothy to alert them to the tragedy, Sara Hutchinson had already seen it reported in the newspapers, and walked over to Grasmere to relate the news. Wordsworth was devastated. 'I have done all in my power to alleviate the distress of poor Dorothy and my Wife, but heaven knows I want consolation myself', he wrote to Richard.[20] The family were cast into deeper distress by John's portrayal in the popular press as an irresponsible captain, and, while most respectable reports of the event suggested that John was not guilty of misconduct, Dorothy and Mary were soon seriously ill with stress. Wordsworth was also emotionally paralysed: 'I feel that there is something cut out of my life which cannot be restored', he wrote.[21] His poetic response to John's death, 'Elegiac Stanzas, Suggested by a Picture of Peele Castle, in a Storm, Painted by George Beaumont' (1806), draws on this idea of irreversible loss, while also indicating Beaumont's role in helping him through this period of grief.

Wordsworth responded to John's death in two key ways. First, his commitment to the idea of community and relationship escalated, his own family now including a daughter Dorothy (always called Dora and born in August 1804), and a son Thomas (born in June 1806). Second, the disaster profoundly affected his poetic style, which became significantly more controlled and regulated. This reserve may also have been a reaction to Coleridge's dismissive behaviour during this period of bereavement. While Wordsworth remained devoted to his friend as the addressee of his philosophic epic, commonly referred to by friends and family as the 'Poem to Coleridge', Coleridge had near abandoned him. He felt painfully jealous of Wordsworth's closeness to Sara and his poetic productivity alike, feelings magnified by the publication of Wordsworth's *Poems, in Two Volumes* (1807). As Coleridge struggled with his addiction to opium, Wordsworth was welcomed into London's literary circles and visited the city to promote his work.

During his trip to London, Wordsworth attended the Royal Academy exhibition in which Beaumont displayed the painting of Piel (or Peele) Castle that inspired 'Elegiac Stanzas'. He was now more intimate with the Beaumonts than Coleridge, and went to stay with them at their new house at Coleorton in Leicestershire. Returning briefly to the capital, where he caught up with his brother Christopher and met the painter John Constable, Wordsworth was soon making plans to go back to the Lakes, taking Mary to Bolton Abbey en route, the site of his new poem 'The White Doe of Rylstone' (1807–8). It was important to the poet that Mary accompanied him on trips to emotionally significant places, and his relationship with her was more loving and affectionate than critics often accept. Only Coleridge in his most invidious and depressed moments inferred that Wordsworth was excessively close to Dorothy, or indeed to Sara, and even he withdrew these accusations in later notebooks and letters.

Many critics have unthinkingly followed Coleridge's resentful reading of Wordsworth's relationship with Mary, but their love-letters, discovered only in 1977, reveal a passionate, mutually dependent and physically ardent bond between the two lovers. As the correspondence illustrates, Wordsworth and Mary consistently express their longing for each other during their marriage: 'when I move I shall feel myself moving towards you … O my beloved how my heart swells at the thought, and how dearly should I have enjoyed being alone with you so long' to 'scc to touch you to speak to you & to hear you speak', he wrote; 'Oh William I cannot tell thee how I love thee & thou must not desire it but feel it, O feel it in the fullness of thy soul & believe that I am the happiest of Wives & Mothers & of all Women the most blessed', Mary replied.[22] Of course Dorothy also adored her brother, exclaiming that she was very 'partial to William' and that he felt a 'sort of violence of Affection' for her too (she notably rejected all her male suitors, including Thomas De Quincey, who, having been rebuffed, predictably implied she was a lesbian).[23] Sara too professed that Wordsworth was 'always the soul of the Parties – the Ladies say they are nothing without him'.[24]

As a gently flirtatious family man, then, Wordsworth was exuberant and lively. As a poet, however, he was self-absorbed and neurotic, fearful that the public would never recognize that the pedagogic foundation of his poetry was to teach them how to feel. The reviews of *Poems, in Two Volumes* had been so negative that he struggled to find a publisher for his new poem 'The White Doe', a point of contention between the poet and his family who were now desperate for financial support. When Coleridge intervened to help him publish the poem, Wordsworth irritably withdrew it, offending an already ill and bitter Coleridge and also demoralizing Dorothy. 'Do, dearest William!' she wrote, 'do pluck up your Courage – overcome your disgust to publishing – It is but a *little trouble*, and all will be over, and we shall be wealthy, and at our ease for one year, at least.'[25] Wordsworth uncharacteristically ignored his sister's pleas, despairing of those 'London wits and witlings' unable to engage with his poetry.[26]

These 'witlings' had damned Wordsworth's recent volumes, bemused by what Lord Byron called their 'puerile' and 'namby-pamby' language. The critic Francis Jeffrey echoed this analysis, claiming that their 'silliness and affectation' renders them 'tedious and affected', 'illegible and unintelligible' and expressive of a 'quintessence of unmeaningness'. The *Satirist* suggested the poems should be jointly published with 'Mother Goose's melodies', while the *Cabinet* thought them 'contemptible effusions', 'trash', 'conceit', 'bombast', a position affirmed also by the *Eclectic Review*, which simply considered them absurd. Even Leigh Hunt, himself later attacked for advocating the effeminate poetics of John Keats and Barry Cornwall, announced in the *Examiner* that Wordsworth join 'The Ancient and Redoubtable Institution of Quacks'.[27]

While critics praised the volumes' sonnets, a more recognizably elite form of poetry, they failed to appreciate the elevation of everyday and domestic feeling in Wordsworth's shorter lyrics. Worse still, their belief that Wordsworth was unable to address philosophical subjects in his poetry both missed the point: the capacity to experience simple feeling enables deep reflection for Wordsworth, and underlies the insight of then-unpublished poems such as 'The Ruined Cottage' (1797) and 'Home at Grasmere' (*c.*1800). Upset by this response to his work, Wordsworth began a series of more meditative pieces in 1808 – 'St Paul's', 'To the Clouds', 'The Tuft of Primroses' – but each was marked by an elegiac caution issuing from that loss of poetic power he described in the 'Elegiac Stanzas'.

It was this loss of power, however, that enabled Wordsworth to articulate the values closest to him – emotional being and community – in prose. His political pamphlet, *The Convention of Cintra* (1809), for example, bemoans Britain's inability to respect the national honour of Spain during the French invasion on 1808. While the British army defeated the French, they then freely allowed them to return home without consequence. This refusal to allow Spain the chance to assert itself over the French paralleled Britain's failure to understand the spirit of liberty behind the American and French Revolutions. Britain was, Wordsworth bemoaned, insensible to the 'moral virtues and qualities of passion which belong to a people' (*PW*, I.235). Perhaps, the poet conjectured, it was this lack of respect for localized communal feeling that made his poetry so unpopular with readers at home.

Wordsworth also addressed his readers' incapacity to imaginatively feel their way into a poem, a political event, or the situation of a neighbour in his *Essays upon Epitaphs* (1809–10), the first of which was published in Coleridge's short-lived magazine, *The Friend*. With his sons Hartley and Derwent, Coleridge was now regularly living with the Wordsworths again, who in May had moved into Allan Bank, a larger house in Grasmere able to accommodate the family and the newly born Catherine. Thomas De Quincey, initially welcomed by the group 'as if he were one of the Family', also joined them there, seemingly replacing Coleridge at least in Dorothy's affections. While she hated the fact that he was still vulnerable to opium ('If he were not under our Roof, he would be just as much the slave of stimulants as ever'), she was more disturbed still by his exploitation of Sara, who was now working day and night on *The Friend*. 'I am hopeless of him,' Dorothy wrote, 'and I dismiss him as much as possible from my thoughts.'[28]

Distressed by the increased distance between Dorothy and Coleridge, Wordsworth turned again to nature, and began work on an intimate travel guide of those landscapes with which he was most familiar. Published first as an introduction to Joseph Wilkinson's *Select Views in Cumberland, Westmore-land, and Lancashire* (1810), Wordsworth later extended it as *A Guide through the District of the Lakes* (1835), appending his earlier essay 'The Sublime and the Beautiful' (1811–12). The Lakes are made sacred here, presented as the ideal backdrop for his vision of community as outlined in poems such as 'Michael' (1800) and 'The Brothers' (1800), and prose pieces such as *The Convention of Cintra* and *Essays upon Epitaphs*. Wordsworth also became a regular teacher at the village school in 1811, enthused by the new curate, William Johnson, who admired his poetry and who was committed to educational reform.

Despite Wordsworth's enthusiasm for local education, the environment and his immediate community, his own relationship with Coleridge had reached crisis point. Coleridge's narcotized dreams were now so paranoid that he fever-ishly believed the Wordsworths were conspiring against him. When Mary gave birth to a fifth child, William, in May 1810, Coleridge went to visit his wife in Keswick, and decided to return to London in October with Montagu who had come up to Allan Bank to see Wordsworth. When Montagu mentioned to Coleridge that Wordsworth had expressed concern over his dependence on opium, he was furious. He broke with Wordsworth for the next eighteen months, writing in his notebook: 'W. authorized M. to tell me, he had no Hope of me! No Hope of me! absol. Nuisance! God's mercy is it a Dream!'[29] Words-worth was so incredulous of the misunderstanding that he refused to register it for the first few months, feeling progressively upset when he realized that their quarrel was the subject of gossip in London. Coleridge, paranoid and dependent on alcohol and opium (despite having left the wife on whom he had blamed his depression for so long), now wrongly believed that Words-worth had used the expression 'rotten drunkard' against him. Their truce was subdued, and, while initiated by Wordsworth, was only settled through a third party, the journalist and writer Henry Crabb Robinson.

No longer close to Coleridge, Wordsworth developed his friendship with Robinson, who introduced him to several admired poets, including Byron, William Lisle Bowles and Anna Barbauld. Wordsworth was also wrapped up in an attempt to secure the release of a French prisoner-of-war distantly related to Annette. Mary supported his involvement and was herself off on a tour of the Wye to see Tintern Abbey. Their letters of this period are more fervent than ever, but while both Mary and Wordsworth were travelling, their three-year old daughter Catherine died of convulsions. Mary, who could not forgive herself for being away, was inconsolable, and spiralled into a depres-sion when 6-year-old Thomas also died of a violent fever only six months later in December 1812. The Wordsworths had been living in their current resi-dence – the disused rectory opposite Grasmere Church – since May 1811, but the close proximity of Catherine and Thomas's graves overpowered Mary to such a degree that, a few months after Thomas's funeral, Wordsworth moved the household to Rydal Mount.

When Coleridge refused to visit during this intense period of bereavement, Wordsworth realized their friendship was irrevocably damaged, and turned all his attention to his family, now in need of serious financial support. Mary's health was failing and Dorothy struggled to look after her sister-in-law and the children, as well as a string of constant visitors, on very little income. When Wordsworth was offered £100 a year from Sir William Lowther, he accepted a salaried post instead. As Distributor of Stamps in Westmorland and the Penrith area of Cumberland, Wordsworth was now responsible for the returns from the stamped, and so taxed, paper used in legal transactions, a position entirely at odds with his poetic aspirations.

Tory humanist?

Many critics denounce Wordsworth for accepting this post, claiming that he had betrayed his vocation and earlier radical politics. While working for the revenue-gathering service undermined Wordsworth's reputation, it is perhaps overly harsh to condemn the poet for taking steps to support his grief-stricken and ailing wife and family. It was Wordsworth, for example, who initiated and contributed to the educational fund for Coleridge's children while their father spent their annuities on opium and spirits. The privileged Byron and Percy Bysshe Shelley may well have ridiculed Wordsworth's choice to work for his money, but real friends of the family understood Wordsworth's reasoning. As one of Dorothy's friends told Robinson: 'It will relieve the females from a good deal of hard work which they have performed most cheerfully – but wh[ich] has certainly at times been prejudicial to them ... and what is the greatest good of all it will release Wordsworths [sic] mind from all anxiety about money.'[30]

Now financially secure, Wordsworth was also free to finally publish a nine-book section of *The Recluse* he called *The Excursion* in 1814. While he was reluctant to publish the epic until it was complete, the death of his children forced Wordsworth to reflect on the uncertainty of his own continued existence; he was also determined to publish something that might overturn the derogatory comments of his critics, Jeffrey and Byron. At the same time, Wordsworth was aware that the poem might potentially feel unduly philosophical to some readers, and so went on holiday to Scotland with Mary and Sara to avoid poring over the initial reviews. As he expected, Jeffrey hated the poem, and even friends like Charles Lamb perceived the poem's religious orthodoxy as one designed to shut down the relationship between God and nature. Wordsworth responded to this particular point by recalling his answer to a question from his son, William: 'How did God make me? Where is God? How does he speak? He never spoke to *me*.' Wordsworth answered that God was a spirit who materialized inside humans as thoughts and emotions, and not an external force.[31]

More disappointing than readers' confusion over the poem's religious message, however, was Coleridge's reaction to the poem. After all, it was Coleridge who had challenged Wordsworth to write the poem in the first place, and now, after years of silence, he accused his friend of failing the task. Wordsworth was again overwhelmed by Coleridge's malice, but it might be easily attributed to his friend's rising celebrity (indicated, for example, by an invitation from the historical painter, Benjamin Haydon, to sit for a life-mask). Undermined by Coleridge's critique, Wordsworth began to obsessively revise and reorder his poems, attempting to rearrange the verses in *Poems, in Two Volumes* (1807) into categories. Reviewers remained critical, however, regarding the classifications as too subjective and the revised preface as sententious. Similar accusations were directed at 'The White Doe of Rylstone' (published in 1815), proclaimed by Jeffrey to be 'the very worst poem we ever saw imprinted in a quarto volume'.[32]

As if all of these bad reviews weren't enough, Wordsworth returned to Rydal Mount to confront a series of tragedies. His brother-in-law, Charles Lloyd, was very ill with a mental disorder exacerbated by the death of his sister; Christopher's wife, Priscilla, had died suddenly after giving birth to a stillborn baby; Mary Lamb was amidst another nervous breakdown leaving Charles Lamb depressed and disaffected; and a wretched De Quincey, broken by his opium addiction, severed all contact with the family after impregnating, and belatedly marrying, his young mistress. More shocking still was the death of Wordsworth's brother, Richard, in May 1816, aged 47 and having only recently, and controversially, married his young servant, Jane Westmorland, with whom he had a 1-year-old son, John.

While mourning Richard's death, Wordsworth and Dorothy discovered that their brother had left the family finances in considerable disarray. Contrary to their assumptions, Richard had lost nearly all of their capital to creditors and in bad investments. Dorothy and Sara were forced to call off their planned trip to Paris to visit Anne-Caroline: Wellington's defeat of Napoleon at the Battle of Waterloo in June 1815 made the trip politically possible, but they could no longer afford it. Meanwhile Wordsworth seemed increasingly disillusioned. His commemorative *Thanksgiving Ode* marking Waterloo warns the British against falling prey to the revolutionary spirit that had haunted France in the

1790s. It is as if, with his family fading around him, Wordsworth turned to what he perceived as the cornerstones of community: national pride, a patriotic education system and moral feeling as conveyed through poetry and an orthodox Church of England Christianity. The *Thanksgiving Ode*, however, signals more than Wordsworth's changed politics. His poetry was becoming more dogmatic, and seemed empty of the touching stories of everyday human life that characterized his more compelling earlier work. Even his *A Letter to a Friend of Robert Burns* (1816), ostensibly an affectionate portrayal of one of Wordsworth's favourite poets, ends up collapsing into an angry and clumsy attack on Jeffrey. He was also upset by the denunciation of several of his poems in Coleridge's literary autobiography, *Biographia Literaria* (1817); when the two men met later in the year, Wordsworth all but ignored him.

The venue for this chilly reunion was a dinner party at Benjamin Haydon's, referred to as the 'Immortal Dinner' because of the array of celebrity guests: Wordsworth, Coleridge, Keats, Lamb and several prominent members of London society. The dinner is especially interesting because of its staging of an interaction between Wordsworth and Keats that casts light on the former's apparently conformist politics. This interaction was prompted by several of Keats' party deciding to cliquishly ridicule one of the less eminent guests, John Kingston. Kingston was one of Wordsworth's bosses at the Stamp Office in London, and when the poet refused to join in the bullying, Keats branded him a cowardly prude.

Defending Kingston against a group of bullies might deem Wordsworth conservative for some, but the act confirms the poet's commitment to tact and fellow feeling. A similar situation arose soon after Haydon's party, when Wordsworth returned home to campaign for the Tory candidates representing Westmorland in the forthcoming general election. While his allegiance appalled Keats, as it did Dorothy, Mary and Sara, it was rooted in a sense of duty to the individuals running for office, the sons of William Lowther who had helped him out of his recent financial troubles. At the same time, Wordsworth's zealous opposition to the liberal Whig candidate, Henry Brougham, can be attributed to the poet's fear that Whig radicalism might spur a repeat of the French Revolution and Britain's war with France.

On the one hand, then, Wordsworth's support of Tory politics amounts to a defence of hereditary wealth and power; but on the other, Wordsworth remained committed to the common man who, in both France and Britain, had been driven to poverty, disaffection and despair as a consequence of a patronizing middle-class politics that could not promise to assist the poor. However we choose to read Wordsworth's involvement in the election, his fervour for the campaign was soon displaced by a return to his poetry, and he published two early poems, *Peter Bell* and *Benjamin the Waggoner*, in 1819. Wordsworth then began to prepare for publication his sonnets on the river Duddon, a short memoir of the local minister Robert Walker called *Topographical Description of the Country of the Lakes*, and some poems about climbing Helvellyn and crossing the Kirkstone Pass. Published in 1820, *The River Duddon: A Series of Sonnets* at last earned Wordsworth critical praise: as the *European Magazine* declared, 'he appears beyond all comparison the most truly sublime, the most touchingly pathetic, the most delightfully simple, the most profoundly philosophical, of all the poetical spirits of the age'.[33] This positive reception encouraged him to issue a four-volume edition, *The Miscellaneous Poems of William Wordsworth* (1820), which not only presented his entire canon but did so in a meticulously revised form.

With his new edition in press, Wordsworth finally travelled back to Calais with Dorothy and Mary with the aim of revisiting the Alps via Belgium, Geneva and Italy. The trip was eventful: Mary met Annette and Anne-Caroline for the first time; and Wordsworth secured an appointment with Helen Maria Williams, to whom he had addressed his first published poem in 1787. The tour also enabled Wordsworth to trace back and reflect on his past, especially as on his way out to Calais he had visited his old walking companion, Robert Jones. On returning to England, Wordsworth also called on Christopher, who had been recently appointed the new Master of Trinity College, Cambridge, and the Beaumonts, with whom he discussed the site of a new local church. Struck by the religious commitment of his friends, Wordsworth began the *Ecclesiastical Sketches* (1822), a group of poems mapping and defending the evolving power of the Church of England against anarchy, revolution and Roman Catholicism. A generous reader might suggest Wordsworth's interest in religious orthodoxy is again an integral part of his relationship with his community: the sketches were, after all, inspired by conversations with the Beaumonts. A more critical reader, however, might agree with Jeffrey that 'The Lake School of Poetry' was 'pretty nearly extinct', a judgement the poet helped realize by not publishing anything new until 1835.[34]

Poet Laureate

By the 1820s, Wordsworth was acknowledged to be one of Britain's leading poets: pirated editions of his work were available in Europe, and the admiration of the Boston minister, William Ellery Channing, and Philadelphia Quaker, Elliot Cresson, secured his reputation in America. During the next few years, many aspiring writers made pilgrimages to Rydal, including Felicia Hemans,

John Stuart Mill, Ralph Waldo Emerson, John Ruskin and Algernon Swinburne. On a visit to Wales in 1824, Wordsworth was warmly received by the Ladies of Llangollen (the intellectual lesbian couple Eleanor Butler and Sarah Ponsonby), and was also visited the following year by the poet Maria Jane Jewsbury, who immediately befriended Dora. Jewsbury, who seemed to reel between the extremes of a morose evangelism and a desire for urban celebrity, was perhaps not the best companion for Dora, however, and Wordsworth decided to part the two women by taking his daughter on a tour of Europe in 1828.

Strangely, Coleridge accompanied them on the tour, although he predictably fell ill during the trip and wrote in his private notebook that he felt alienated from Wordsworth, whose 'hard, rigid, continual, in all points despotic Egotism' and 'coarse concerns about money' left 'the flowers of his genius ... faded and withered'.[35] Wordsworth had, in fact, become obsessed with the publication and presentation of his poetry at the expense of writing new work, and even Dorothy admitted that she feared *The Recluse* would never be written.[36] Her brother seemed more invested in leaving his legacy to future readers: a five-volume *The Poetical Works of William Wordsworth* appeared in 1827; Edward Moxon's *Selections from the Poems of William Wordsworth, Esq., Chiefly for the Use of Schools and Young Persons* was printed in 1831; a collected sonnets appeared in 1838; he worked on *The Prelude* throughout 1839; and also had plans to issue a cheap edition for the common reader.

Even when Wordsworth did publish new work in his volume *Yarrow Revisited, and Other Poems* (1835), it was in part a response to two earlier verses, *Yarrow Unvisited* (1807) and *Yarrow Visited* (included in the 1815 *Poems*). The volume's postscript attacking the Poor Law Amendment Act (1834) at least confirms Wordsworth's continued commitment to the poor: the act cut off any relief to the labouring classes, forcing them into workhouses instead. Wordsworth is still considered politically conservative at this time, however, because of his opposition to the Catholic Emancipation Act (1829) and Reform Bill (1832). Yet these views too derived from a desire to protect the poor against the kind of revolutionary activities that had desolated rural France. Wordsworth also defended Rydal against enclosure in 1824, and battled with the Kendal and Windermere Railway company's plan to ravage the rural communities of the Vales of Rydal and Grasmere. Modern critics might ignore Wordsworth's service to the poor in this period, but contemporaries did not. During his speech celebrating Wordsworth's honorary doctorate of civil law from the University of Oxford in 1839, the theologian and poet John Keble applauded Wordsworth as the nation's greatest poet of the poor.

However we read Wordsworth's late political position, then, it emerges from a sustained emotional relationship to labouring communities. By contrast, the younger, and notably wealthier, generation of poets that so derided his apparent defection from radicalism aligned themselves with politics as much for reasons of fashion as of belief. As Wordsworth wrote of the 'radical' publisher John Murray, for example, who declined to answer any of his letters: 'he is too great a Personage for any one but a Court, an Aristocratic or most fashionable Author to deal with'.[37] Always unconcerned with style (a notorious outfit included 'striped duck trousers' and 'fustian gaiters'), Wordsworth wrote about what he genuinely considered important, even if this meant addressing awkward subjects like capital punishment: his infamous *Sonnets upon the Punishment of Death* (1841) are discussed in Chapter 3.

Now in his late sixties, Wordsworth undoubtedly wrote some maverick verses, but his relationships with friends and family remained steady. In 1837, he travelled to France and Italy with Henry Crabb Robinson, revisiting places that revived emotionally significant memories. While stunned by St Peter's in Rome, he was more affected by a large pine tree that he discovered was being preserved by a subsidy from his now deceased friend, George Beaumont. The specificity of the tree as a symbol of Beaumont's kindness registered more deeply than the grandeur of buildings or art for Wordsworth. Similarly, the Italian Lakes felt meaningful to him because they provoked vivid memories of his tour there with Dorothy, who was now suffering from a form of Alzheimer's disease that confined her to the Rydal Mount household. Remembering how healthy Dorothy had been during their early travels together moved Wordsworth so much that he was forced to keep 'much to myself, and very often could I, for my heart's relief, have burst into tears'.[38]

Reflecting on Dorothy's illness made Wordsworth suddenly aware of how fragile his personal community had become. Coleridge passed away in London in 1834, refusing to see his wife, children or friends in his final days of illness; and Sara Hutchinson died of rheumatic fever the year after. On reading about the death of the poet and novelist James Hogg, Wordsworth wrote an elegy called 'Extempore Effusion', in which he grieves for his friends (Walter Scott, Charles Lamb, Robert Jones and Felicia Hemans were also recently deceased), as well as his own transience in the world. In addition to Dorothy's collapse and the varying illnesses of those close to him, Wordsworth felt betrayed and saddened by the secret marriage of his daughter Dora to the poet and translator Edward Quillinan in 1841.

Even towards the end of his life, however, Wordsworth was still forming deep attachments to new friends. One such acquaintance was an admirer called Isabella Fenwick, who first visited Rydal Mount in 1833, soon becoming an affectionately loved friend of Wordsworth, Mary and Robinson. Moving to Ambleside in 1838 to be near the Wordsworths, she was called on daily by the poet, who in 1843 dictated a series of notes to her on the composition of his poems. The 'Fenwick Notes' remain a valuable record for readers of Wordsworth's late views on his poetry and career.[39]

Wordsworth was also consoled by the continued rise of his reputation. He sat for portraits (painted by the artists Francis Wilkin, William Boxall, John Gardner and Haydon), and was granted honorary memberships from the Royal Institution of Liverpool and the University of Durham. He was also asked to present the 'Newdigate Prize', an award for best poem by an undergraduate, to a young John Ruskin, and at breakfast the next day met several members of the 'Oxford Movement' (discussed in Chapter 2). The party was hosted by Francis Faber, whose brother Frederick was an established admirer of Wordsworth. Moving to Ambleside to assist a local clergyman, Frederick soon sought to claim Wordsworth for the Oxford Movement, and had a significant effect on some of the religiously inclined revisions the poet made to the *Ecclesiastical Sketches*, *Adventures on Salisbury Plain* and even his new *Musings near Aquapendente* (1837; 1841).

After a long wait, Wordsworth was finally appointed Poet Laureate in 1843. He resigned his role as Distributor of Stamps and settled into literary fame. Yet he was haunted by the thought that his life had 'been in a great measure wasted' and sat, Mary admitted to Fenwick, 'more over the fire in silence etc etc and is sooner tired on his walks'.[40] While he had managed to put together one last volume of his works, *Poems, Chiefly of Early and Late Years* (1845), he had been crushed by a series of terrible deaths: Mary's sister Joanna in 1843; his grandson Edward in 1845; both his brother Christopher and nephew John in 1846; Haydon's suicide in the same year; and most shocking of all, his beloved Dora in 1847. Despite the constant flow of admiring visitors to Rydal, Wordsworth would often, Mary wrote, 'retire to his room sit alone & cry incessantly', avoiding anywhere that reminded him of Dora. Attempting to rally him from this depression, his nephew Christopher began to collect memoranda for a future biography, published in 1851 as a two-volume *Memoirs of William Wordsworth*. While the poet's health suddenly revived in 1849, enabling him to cross 'the Malvern Hill twice without suffering any inconvenience', reported Robinson, he succumbed to pleurisy in 1850 and died at midday on 23 April. Dorothy died five years later, and Mary, who published *The Prelude* for her husband on his death, passed away in 1859. Both women were buried next to Wordsworth at Grasmere.

Chapter 2

Contexts

Wordsworth is a deeply contradictory figure: a confident and opinionated thinker who was often paralysed by self-doubt; a radical who sympathized with the Tory politics of England's elite; an Anglican churchgoer who proclaimed to his 'Great God! I'd rather be / A Pagan'; and a deeply loved and supported man who valued community but locked himself into periods of loneliness and grief.[1] The subject of human feeling, however, consistently engaged his attention, and his poetry is a record of his various attempts to translate the emotional content of lived experiences into poetic form. He does this, not to evoke sympathy, but to teach readers how to think about their own feelings. In doing so, Wordsworth sought to reframe ideas about sensibility and sympathy current during his lifetime as a way of exploring the relationship between individual feeling (what he personally felt) and collective emotion (feelings shared by particular groups or communities).

This chapter explores these debates alongside the historical and cultural context that informed Wordsworth's thinking about nature, politics, gender and religion, themes that change as Britain was steadily propelled into an industrialized capitalism. The consequences of this technological destruction of the landscape, particularly through the process of 'enclosure', were famine, conflict and alienation. Wordsworth's early poetry, examined in Chapter 4, attends to the increasing number of marginal wanderers displaced from their communities by these conditions. The discussion here aims to give the reader contextual points of departure from which to read this and Wordsworth's later poetry, interwoven as it is with reflections on the Enlightenment, nature, the revolution debates, imperialism, community and religion.

The Enlightenment

What is known as the Enlightenment signifies the promotion of rational thinking in the eighteenth century; thinking that endorsed culture and reason, rather than nature or religion, as the grounds for solving problems and conflicts. Logical argument, and not intuitive feeling, was thus promoted as the spring of liberalism, tolerance and moral virtue. Wordsworth struggled with these ideas because he believed that one could only learn what it means to be human through a relationship with nature. The term 'nature' for Wordsworth meant more than the non-urban and rural, however: it connoted what he perceived as the 'natural' aspects of us, those intuitions, feelings and passions that make us 'human'. An animating force that impels us to attend to situations through love and sympathy, rather than calculation or analysis, nature for Wordsworth also held the capacity to protect and redeem us from interactions with culture.

Wordsworth worried that the Enlightenment might make people overly dependent on cold reason by expelling feeling from political and social life. He wrote poetry to reveal the extraordinary and mystical elements of the commonplace routines of daily human life. The Enlightenment, on the other hand, concerned itself with obvious achievements, in science, medicine, political reform, economics, publishing, consumerism and religion, as well as in literature and art. One could argue that this commitment to progress and toleration promoted the kind of respect and affection for others that Wordsworth too advocated. Yet he was ultimately a 'counter-Enlightenment' poet because of his distaste for the idea that human life is a straightforward journey of advancement and discovery: living, he argued, was a process of accidents, chance happenings and arbitrary events that could not be explained in any simply rational way.

Wordsworth was particularly suspicious of the Enlightenment's impulse to analyse and categorize. The philosopher, psychologist and scientist, David Hartley, for example, followed Enlightenment logic in attempting to assess human feeling through materialist science. In his *Observations on Man* (1749), Hartley argued that human ideas derive from physical sensations ('feelings') that cause vibrations in the nerves. These vibrations are in turn transmitted to the brain where they spark ideas through 'association'. The philosophy of 'association' proposes that we feel a sensation, make sense of it by associating it with previous sense-based experiences, make a value judgement about it, and then express this judgement in language. Hartley argued that positive vibrations produce ethical and liberal ideas, while negative vibrations cause corrupt and depraved thoughts. While Wordsworth was concerned that these kind of scientific ideas were 'a succedaneum' (*P*, II.219), or substitute for thinking about nature, Hartley argued that science connected us back with nature and also to the divine. For Hartley, God himself made an 'affective impression' on the human body, our feelings granted by God to remind us of his existence.

Coleridge was originally captivated by Hartley's theories and named his first son after him. He shared his enthusiasm for Hartley with the philosopher and scientist Joseph Priestley, who was also a 'dissenter': someone whose views departed from the political and religious ideologies of the day. In an attempt to undermine current religious orthodoxy in Britain, Priestley republished Hartley's *Observations*, arguing that the study offered a template for reconciling Christian belief with the disciplines of physiology, neurology, psychology and metaphysics. Priestley received his own education from a 'Dissenting Academy', one of the educationally progressive colleges instituted in the 1660s to instruct dissenting ministers. By the eighteenth century, dissenting academies had become famous for their radical syllabi, consisting of languages, classics, astronomy, civil law, philosophy and history, through to pneumatics, magnetism and accounting. Having encountered Hartley in his studies at Daventry Academy, Priestley went on to teach modern languages and rhetoric at Warrington Academy and famously discovered oxygen gas there in 1774. A model Enlightenment thinker, he was drawn to Hartley as someone who brought together reason with feeling, a theorist, Priestley argued, who could both 'enlighten the mind' and 'improve the heart'.[2]

Wordsworth was drawn to Priestley's reading of Hartley, but was not sure it was right. Critics of Hartley declared that his ideas had ushered in a very practical scientific revolution, consisting of subjects such as chemistry, optics, electromagnetism and biology, all dependent on material observation and experiment. Empirical science, it was feared, would threaten to replace God with pragmatic fact, deifying scientists while dehumanizing people as 'atoms' and 'matter'. Priestley at least had tried to argue that all 'matter' contained an internal, divine force that fuelled material, as well as mental and spiritual, activity. Likewise, the chemist Humphry Davy argued in his 1802 Royal Institution lectures that the advantages of science went beyond material progression, and provided an important stimulus to the imagination.[3] Wordsworth was impressed by Davy's application of science to social life and the creation of art, and in turn, Davy claimed that the political and psychological force of the *Lyrical Ballads* (1798) had inspired his work.

Indeed the link between science and politics was widely regarded as revolutionary. For Priestley, the gaseous and explosive terminology associated with chemistry offered a politically, as well as scientifically, militant language through which to express dissenting ideals. 'We are', he declared in 1787, 'laying gunpowder, grain by grain, under the old building of error and superstition, which a single spark may hereafter inflame so as to produce an instantaneous explosion.'[4] The politician Edmund Burke declared in the House of Commons that the statement was tantamount to sedition, and the following year, an anti-dissenting mob burned down Priestley's Birmingham home, laboratory and two local dissenting chapels, persuading the scientist to emigrate.

Burke's anxiety about Priestley was as much to do with his claim to the freedom of speech as with the content of his argument. Conservatives were increasingly nervous about an emergent liberalism that endorsed universal access to ideas previously discussed only by the rich and powerful. The modern philosopher Jürgen Habermas argues that this access was made possible by the formation of the 'public sphere', physical spaces in which private people could 'come together as a public' to discuss views newly learned from an increasingly available market of books and periodicals.[5] Chapels and coffee houses were transformed into centres of literary, political, religious and philosophical discussion where tradesmen, shopkeepers and gentlemen alike could debate the news and ideas of the day and in doing so freely form 'public' opinion. Embracing Enlightenment ideology, this 'public' implicitly sanctioned the development of national and international industries (textiles, the metal industry and paper production, for example), while also arguing for working rights and 'fair-trade' production.

Overseen by the Enlightenment principles of reason and rationality, rather than state or religious authority, the public sphere hypothetically included everyone. In Scotland, for example, new and progressive ideas rapidly circulated through clubs and societies, as well as the forward-thinking universities of Edinburgh and Glasgow. The Scottish philosopher David Hume, suggested that the most meaningful political theories evolved, not in parliament, but through conversation, in coffee houses and debating clubs, journals and newspapers. Birmingham's Lunar Society, London's Club of Honest Whigs and Manchester's Philosophical Society were all modelled on Hume's advancement of debate and exchange as the foundation for intellectual and political expansion.

In practice, however, the public sphere excluded children, women and non-propertied men, the subjects of many of Wordsworth's poems. England's public sphere was especially closed, dominated as it was by an ideology of reason that Wordsworth argued could justify social evolution in theory while ignoring the particularities of individual groups or people in practice. For example, the state claimed to have passed the Seditious Societies Act (1799) to regulate the dissemination of dangerous reading material. In demanding the compulsory registration of printing presses, however, the Act insisted that publications carry the name of the printer, so enabling the prosecution of those involved with the dissemination of radical literature. Moreover, while the so-called 'public sphere' claimed to promote cross-class exchange, it in fact only allowed aristocrats to mix with bourgeois intellectuals. Wordsworth had no interest in such circles, and perceived human existence not as a series of cumulative achievements, but as the daily feelings individuals experienced. While the individuals he presents in his poetry are commonly isolated, ruined, bewildered and alienated, they are also images of stillness; they find solace, not in progress, but in their immediate environment and the feelings they attach to it.

Nature and the land

This environment was under considerable threat from Enlightenment ideology in the eighteenth century, the force of industrial and economic change granting little respect to the countryside or its rural inhabitants. The compulsion of 'Getting and spending', as Wordsworth wrote in his sonnet 'The World Is Too Much with Us' (published in 1807), had infected British society with greed and unrealizable desire, creating a society of individuals now 'out of tune' with nature (2, 8). The shift into this culture of greed was set in motion by the newly embraced capitalist mode of production, which flourished under a rhetoric of 'improvement'. 'Improvement' referred to both the tending of land to make it more profitable, as well as to the people who laboured to manage the land. While the idea of 'cultivating' people was offensive to Wordsworth, he was also appalled by the idea that nature could be 'improved' upon. The Board of Agriculture (1793) disagreed, draining bogs and fens and converting arable to pasture land to make the countryside both more workable and more aesthetically pleasing.

'Improvement' meant recasting the countryside in accordance with the aesthetic convention of the 'picturesque', one that deliberately reproduced the rusticity of the landscape in an artificial or virtual manner. The propertied elite who populated London-based courts, offices of state and parliament, for example, bought up land previously owned by the local community and then landscaped it into private parks for their personal enjoyment. Privatized land thus served as a refuge for the rich from the self-absorbed reality of metropolitan life, but also made money as land that could be farmed and worked on. Accordingly, landscapers like Richard Payne Knight, Lancelot 'Capability' Brown and Humphrey Repton recreated a bucolic naturalism enhanced by simulated ruins but with the vagrants and rural dwellers who had previously lived there airbrushed out. Sir Uvedale Price, for example, a major proponent of the picturesque, argued for its aesthetic in his *An Essay on the Picturesque* (1794–8) while debarring labourers from collecting fuel from his now pristine property. Wordsworth attacked landowners like Price in his portrayal of 'Harry Gill' in the *Lyrical Ballads*, who, deep in the middle of winter, evicts the dispossessed and impoverished 'Goody Blake'. The erasure of the human element of the landscape troubled Wordsworth as much as its regulation by reductive aesthetic categories.

Wordsworth was, however, drawn to the concept of the 'sublime' because it described the emotional and imaginative impressions that nature effected on the individual rather than the landscape itself. The sublime was introduced into the aesthetic debates of the period by Nicolas Boileau's translation of Longinus' first-century *On the Sublime* (1736). For Longinus, the sublime suggests that the individual has the capacity to transcend the limits of the human condition through his or her intellectual and emotional willingness to explore the mysterious and unexplained. Edmund Burke updated Longinus in *A Philosophical Inquiry into the Origin of our Ideas of the Sublime and the Beautiful* (1757), arguing that human knowledge is derived from sense experiences organized by the imagination into impressions. The mind does not create anything new, but only reflects on what the imagination perceives. He argued that the sublime is triggered by vast and vertiginous objects (a mountain, a precipice), which astonish and terrify the imagination into a state of fear and unreason. As the individual's composure is shattered, he or she undergoes a feeling of paralysis and blockage before being suddenly rushed on by a whirling 'irresistible force' that gradually recedes to leave a feeling of renewal.[6]

Like Burke, Wordsworth understood 'the body of this sensation' (*PW*, II.351) as one made up of sense perception (we observe the form of the sublime object), sense duration (we take our time viewing the object to properly receive 'a sense of sublimity'), and sense impression (we respect the affective and powerful blow this effects on our minds and bodies). In his essay on the sublime, Wordsworth asks readers to imaginatively 'look up' at the 'Pikes of Langdale' in Windermere and the 'black precipice contiguous to them' so that they might feel the grandeur of such a vision and then stay with it: as he writes in 'Tintern Abbey' (1798), such an experience transforms what is being looked at into something 'Felt in the blood, and felt along the heart' (29) before passing into the mind.

The power awakened in us by the sublime, Wordsworth argues, also 'rouses us to a sympathetic energy & calls upon the mind to grasp at something towards which it can make approaches but which it is incapable of attaining', whether this be 'of a spiritual nature, as that of the Supreme Being', or of a human nature (*PW*, II.354). The sublime thus gives us access to ideas and emotions we would otherwise find incomprehensible. Wordsworth intimates this in his ballad 'The Solitary Reaper', written about a woman harvesting grain and singing to herself whom he came upon during his tour of Scotland in 1803. While he cannot understand the meaning of her song (she sings in Gaelic), he nevertheless listens with his heart and mind, moved by the sublime impact her voice has upon him.

More urgent than any aesthetic debate, however, was 'enclosure', a process that privatized more than 4 million acres of once collectively owned pasturage. Between 1762 and 1844, over 2,500 enclosure acts were passed that in effect robbed rural workers and the poor of the land they commonly worked on. Like picturesque landscaping, enclosure purported to tidy up this 'common' or 'waste' land by the planting of naturalized hedgerows. In reality, enclosure sliced the land up into hemmed-in strips that could be privately farmed by those wealthy enough to bid for the seized land. Once purchased, the land-owner would deny rural labourers access unless they had become his employees. This was devastating for the rural poor, who had previously relied on what are called 'customary rights', such as 'estover' (wood-gathering); 'piscary' (fishing); 'turbary' (peat-cutting); and 'gleaning' (picking up stray stalks of wheat after the harvest had been gathered).

When these customary rights were criminalized, many labourers felt disinherited from their own land, and responded by destroying fences and hedgerows and burning ricks of hay and corn. As food prices soared and famine set in, especially during Britain's war with France, rioting became more frequent, building up to the Captain Swing riots of 1830–1 in which hundreds of rural communities mobilized to protest against their disenfranchised status. Radicals like Thomas Spence had already argued in his 'Land Plan' (1775) that wealth earned off the land should be equally distributed back among the community who had once communally owned it; while Thomas Paine insisted in his *Agrarian Justice* (1796) that farmers, at the very least, had responsibilities to the communities who had been unjustifiably evicted from the land that once supported them. Dispersed to rural labourers by a middle-class and city-based reform movement, these ideas helped encourage demands for an increase in wages and poor relief, a reduction of taxes on essential commodities such as food, and also government recognition of the widespread unemployment caused by new technologies.

By the early nineteenth century, the 'Speenhamland' system was introduced, named after the town in which the policy was made law, and serving to add to the wages of labourers according to the price of bread and the number of their dependants. But the imposition of a level of minimum subsistence forced down the wages of many labourers, while at the same time driving wanderers and beggars into workhouses. The disenfranchised, sick and old were thus locked away within squalid and cramped institutions that dehumanized the inmates, imposing on them horrific sanitation and health conditions.

Wordsworth was alarmed by the futility of these reforms, enforced by city-based intellectuals completely removed from the lived experiences of the labouring classes. His poem 'The Old Cumberland Beggar' (1798), for example, suggests that poor-relief schemes enslave the most deprived individuals in society by tying them to a subsistence law that then strips them of customary rights. That which is customary or habitual is not just an entitlement for Wordsworth's balladic figures; it is the very thing that guides them through a life that would make no sense if scrutinized through the lens of rational reflection. The narrator insists that neither the local community nor the nation's economists need respond directly to the beggar, who in turn has no responsibility to the villagers who offer him basic provisions. What matters in the poem is not charity but attention, the narrator's reverence towards the beggar underlining the care and watchfulness with which the beggar is observed by him, the villagers and us as readers. Refusing to regard the beggar as a problem, then, his community lets him get on with the life he has, rather than imposing a moral sense of the life they think he should have. 'As in the eye of Nature he has lived', the narrator declares, 'So in the eye of Nature let him die' (188–9).

Revolution and social change

If the poor were being left desolate by enclosure, they were plunged into still greater destitution by the impact of Britain's continued war with France. The two countries had been at war since 1689, each driven by a desire for religious and colonial power. Since the ascension of the fiercely Protestant William III, Britain had opposed France's Catholic affiliations. During the eighteenth century, the two countries struggled to gain political and religious control of the Americas and Asia, a clash that fuelled what is now called the Seven Years War (1756–63). Britain's opposition to the French Revolution of 1789 engendered further conflict, initially with the new Republic and then with the First Empire of Napoleon. Having finally defeated France at the Battle of Waterloo (1815), Britain was financially broken and politically divided, especially as many British reformers sympathized with France as a model of democracy and equality.

Wordsworth was introduced to many liberal republicans at university and was inspired to visit France because of a pro-revolutionary politics engendered by the London Revolutionary Society. Previous attempts to revolutionize Britain, however, had failed, ending either in stalemate or extreme violence. The Gordon Riots (1780), for example, had been led through London by the radical Lord George Gordon to protest against poverty and the passing of the pro-Roman Catholic Papists Act (1778). More property was damaged during these riots than in Paris during the whole Revolution, and while several rioters were arrested for High Treason, some were executed. Horrified by this outcome, radicals like the political philosopher and dissenting chaplain, Richard Price, openly saluted the idea of revolution. He praised both the American Revolution (1775–83), in which North America overthrew British colonial rule to declare their independence as a new nation; and also the French Revolution, which had abolished an absolute monarchy dependent on a corrupt nobility and Catholic Church. For Price, America and France were models of reform, and had kindled a revolutionary 'blaze that lays despotism in ashes and warms and illuminates Europe!'[7]

The French Revolution in particular astonished those in Britain, sympathizers and adversaries alike. Tension had been escalating in France in 1789, and when a general assembly was convened in May to address the nation's financial crisis, many French people felt that royalty and the nobility had usurped governance. On 14 July, a large group of demonstrators stormed the Bastille prison, both because it was a symbol of monarchical control, and also because of the arms and ammunition stored inside. When the French army fired on the protestors, they responded by dragging the prison's governor into the streets, decapitating him and then parading his head, fixed onto a pike, through the streets of Paris.

Sensitive to these levels of anger, the liberal members of the Assembly drew up a document of equality called the *Declaration of the Rights of Man* (1791), which implied church reform, the abolition of feudalism and economic freedom for the rural classes. These liberals, however, soon split into two factions. On one side were the 'Girondists', named after a region in southwest France with which many of their supporters were associated. The Girondists promoted a patriotic and relatively nonviolent form of democratic revolution that was supported by political intellectuals such as Jacques Pierre Brissot and Thomas Paine. On the other side were the 'Jacobins', named after the Jacobin Club in Paris where they met. This group were headed by the extreme radicals Maximilien Robespierre and Jean-Paul Marat, and were ready to employ physical force to realize their ideals. While both groups supported the arrest of King Louis XVI in 1792, the Girondists wished to keep him hostage to secure continued debate, whereas the Jacobins instigated popular support for his immediate execution. By contrast with the Jacobins, the Girondists suddenly seemed faint-hearted, and Parisians sided with Robespierre, cheering as Louis was guillotined in January 1793 for high treason and crimes against the state.

Robespierre's plan to lethally remove those opposed to the conservation of the Republic was also initially very popular. The Revolutionary Tribunal ordered the execution of anyone holding suspicious political opinions or clerical sympathies, and more than 40,000 people were killed during the ensuing 'Reign of Terror'. When Robespierre attempted to institute his own form of state religion, however, members within the Assembly, now horrified by the rising violence, conspired to overthrow the Jacobins, who were themselves guillotined in July 1794. The coup instigated a further 'White Terror', killing hundreds of Jacobins under the pretence of attempting to re-establish the liberal, constitutional values proposed back in 1789. At the same time, the Jacobin sympathizer and military commander, Napoleon Bonaparte, was leading the French army into brutal conflicts across Europe. He returned to France in 1799 to direct a coup against the current Constitution. Imposing his own law, Napoleon assumed the lifetime position of First Consul later that year, and his reconciliatory efforts with the Catholic Church and implementation of civil law effectively brought an end to the French Revolution.

The impact of these events on British politics was monumental. Radicals were excited that a people-led revolution had succeeded, but were then sickened by the ensuing terror; conservatives damned the whole affair as an example of the consequences of extending rights beyond the aristocracy. The Revolution also provoked a pamphlet war between radicals and conservatives that included many of the most significant publications of the Romantic period. The conservative Burke commenced the debate by damning Richard Price as an infidel intent on resurrecting the enthusiasm that had led to the Gordon Riots. His *Reflections on the Revolution in France* (1790) prophetically outlined the implications of advancing claims of natural rights and liberty against the order of society: 'Laws overturned; tribunals subverted; industry without vigour; commerce expiring; the revenue unpaid, yet the people impoverished; a church pillaged, and a state not relieved; civil and military anarchy made the constitution of the kingdom ... There must be blood', he foresaw.[8]

Burke's *Reflections* sold 30,000 copies in the first two years of publication and prompted over 200 works supporting its loyalist position and over 100 works questioning its commitments. Thomas Paine's *The Rights of Man* (1791; 1792) was among the texts that opposed Burke, ultimately eclipsing it by selling over 200,000 copies in its first three years. Paine's pamphlet moored revolutionary debate firmly in the public domain because of the way readers disseminated its ideas in street literature, ballads, graffiti, parodies and caricatures. Paine undermined Burke's insistence that absolute government control was necessitated because of the depraved nature of humanity by arguing that the precedent for this idea was William of Normandy's invasion of England in 1066. Calling for an alliance with America and France, Paine asserted the idea of a collective democratic government that would protect the free rights of all individuals, taxing the wealthy to support the poor, destitute and elderly. Mary

Wollstonecraft anticipated these arguments in *A Vindication of the Rights of Men* (1790), reminding Burke that rights are granted by God, not tradition. She followed her success with *A Vindication of the Rights of Woman* (1792), which directly refuted the French National Assembly's proposal that women remain uneducated and stay distanced from the dangers of political or intellectual revolution.

Wollstonecraft prioritized the importance of individual judgement for men and women, a premise later taken up by her future husband, William Godwin. Godwin claimed that his *Enquiry Concerning Political Justice and Its Influence on Modern Morals and Happiness* (1793) was a sequel to Paine's *The Rights of Man*, arguing as it did for a utilitarian moral theory rooted in the rational influence of truth on the human mind. An assertion of the goodness of humanity in the wake of the French 'Terror', Godwin's enquiry sought to reform society through reasoned reflection and was immediately popular with those looking for philosophical direction, such as Wordsworth and Coleridge.

Having witnessed the first anniversary of the storming of the Bastille at first hand with his friend Robert Jones, Wordsworth had returned to London just as the 'paper wars' had begun, eager to read the 'master Pamphlets of the day' (*P*, IX.97). His own contribution to this debate, *A Letter to the Bishop of Llandaff* (1793), was a response to Bishop Richard Watson's portrayal of the Revolution as a marker of savage irrationality. Indicating his familiarity with Burke and Paine, Wordsworth wrote the letter to expose his support for a French republic based on ideals of reform and defend Louis's execution. Like animals just released from their cages, Wordsworth argues, the French people may well have acted excessively at first, but once granted their freedom, will settle into a moderate and happy mode of being. Richard begged his brother not to publish the pamphlet, reminding him that 'by the suspension of the Habeas Corpus acts the Ministers have great powers'.[9] Wordsworth acquiesced: the Royal Proclamation against Seditious Writings and Publications (1792) had already been used to prosecute Thomas Paine for libel; and the cessation of Habeas Corpus had allowed the government to detain several intellectuals, including Coleridge's friend John Thelwall, under treasonous charges of 'imagining the king's death'.[10]

The government's continued attempts to suppress radicalism in legislative enactments (a series of laws collectively known as the 'gagging acts') may also have dissuaded Wordsworth from publishing his journal the *Philanthropist*. Yet Wordsworth was also beginning to change his mind about the Revolution, partly because of meeting Coleridge. By contrast with the passionate and faithful Coleridge, Godwin's cold and abstract rationalism seemed frighteningly close to the ideals driving Robespierre's 'Terror'. Wordsworth had always supported the Revolution because of his personal experiences in France, dismayed as he had been by the extreme rural poverty caused by French aristocratic greed. Yet on returning to Paris in October 1792 when the Terror was at its height, Wordsworth was horrified at the social turmoil he saw potentially spreading to Britain. A city that had once represented political hope to the poet, Paris now seemed 'a place of fear, / Unfit for the repose of night, / Defenceless as a wood where tigers roam' (*P*, X.80–3).

'Confounded' by 'ghastly visions' of 'despair' at the revolution's decline into 'tyranny', Wordsworth concluded that human beings might not be innately good at all (*P*, X.374–5). Yet unlike Godwin, who sought to regulate people through reason, or Burke, who gave up hope on humanity altogether, Wordsworth still believed that humans are always saved from self-interest by their relationships with others. He personally had found redemption both in Coleridge's friendship and in the visionary politics he promoted; Coleridge renewed Wordsworth's belief in the imagination as the motor of a political protest effectively communicated in poetry. After reading Godwin, Wordsworth had written *The Borderers* (1796–7), a play in which a cynical villain is sadistically driven by intellectual power; his friendship with Coleridge, on the other hand, inspired 'The Ruined Cottage' (1797), a poem which elevates the spontaneous blessings offered by nature and human benevolence to those shattered by the social effects of war. Wordsworth realized that revolution would not help this underclass after all, but in fact created a bloodbath provoking wider global military conflict.

Despite Wordsworth's early love affair with France, by 1803 he had enlisted with the Grasmere volunteers to fight against Napoleon. 'Surely there never was a more determined hater of the French,' Dorothy now wrote of her brother, 'nor one more willing to do his utmost to destroy them if they really do come.'[11] Like Dorothy, most people assumed Britain was under constant threat of invasion by the French from the late 1790s. This fear was exacerbated by the government's inability to finance the war, a problem it attempted to solve by increasing taxes, but which then led to serious food rioting in both 1794–6 and 1799–1801. When Wordsworth sent a copy of the *Lyrical Ballads* to the liberal Whig Charles James Fox in 1801, he wanted to prove that the imagination might effect greater social change than organized military force ever could. Poetry, he believed, had the capacity not only to highlight problems such as 'the spreading of manufactures', 'heavy taxes', the institution of 'workhouses' and 'Soup-shops', but was also able to restore the emotional being of those stripped of it both abroad and at home.[12]

The counter-revolutionary climate in which the *Lyrical Ballads* sought to call attention to the plight of the rural classes ironically ensured a subdued response to the volume. While the poems seemed much stranger than the political ballads so popular with readers at the time, they also threatened to stir up potentially revolutionary feeling. The economic crisis that followed the Duke of Wellington's defeat of Napoleon at Waterloo in 1815, however, rendered parliamentary reform more urgent than ever, and the consequent debate finally led to the Reform Act of 1832. Yet the Bill did little more than alleviate the anxieties of Whig liberals regarding electoral inequities, leaving more than 70 per cent of adult men without the vote and populating parliament with middle-class property owners as wary of revolution as their predecessors.

Imperialism and colonialism

Poverty and social unrest worsened in the late eighteenth century, largely because of enclosure. Yet the process of enclosure had been encouraged by Britain's imperial project abroad, one founded on the forced seizure of land. As the President of the Board of Agriculture, Sir John Sinclair, declared: 'Let us not be satisfied with the liberation of Egypt, or the subjugation of Malta, but let us subdue Finchley Common; let us conquer Hounslow Heath, let us compel Epping Forest to submit to the yoke of improvement.'[13] The rhetoric of 'improvement' had long been employed to justify the expansion of British imperialism, disingenuously presented as offering indigenous people hope of relief from disease and famine through financing – but then exploiting – self-sufficient farming practices.

The expansion of the British Empire had been entirely sustained by black slavery. Sugar from the Caribbean, tobacco from Chesapeake, rice from South Carolina, cotton from the West Indies, coffee from the Yemen, chocolate from Aztec Mexico and tea from Canton were all imported into Britain by white slavers. Around 3 million slaves were transported from Africa to Britain's colonies during the eighteenth century, many of them unable to survive slave-ship conditions, let alone manual labour on plantations, and natural increases in the slave population were severely inhibited by problems of infertility and mortality brought on by inhumane mistreatment. At the same time, mercantile demands for slaves grew as Britain consumed more and more quantities of sweet tea (37 million pounds of tea was imported in 1750, and 240,000 tons of sugar in 1800).

Locked into counter-revolutionary conservatism, however, Britain was not prepared to grant slave workers rights or representation. In Quebec, the Cape, Ceylon and Trinidad, for example, power was held by a royally appointed governor who represented the British Crown. He enforced rule by self-appointing local assemblies and was helped further by Anglican churches and schools, newly established to provide religious instruction to British settlers and the local community. While imperial administrators were wary of imposing Anglicanism on both the non-Christian native population and dissenting European settlers, they perhaps did not foresee that by converting the colonies to Christianity they were effectively granting them equality under the eyes of God. Christians at home could not condone the exploitation of their spiritual brothers and sisters, and in 1787, a group of Quakers formed a committee in London to demand an end to the Atlantic slave trade. Much to the surprise of the government, the abolitionist cause was widely subscribed to by the middle classes as well as by artisans and working men and women; following the campaign of William Wilberforce, the slave trade was abolished in 1806–7.

Like many poets of the period, Wordsworth protested against the slave trade, arguing in *A Letter to the Bishop of Llandaff*: 'Slavery is a bitter and poisonous draught; we have but one consolation under it – that a nation may dash the cup to the ground when she pleases' (*PW*, I.36). The critic Alan Bewell also argues that the poetic experiments attempted in the *Lyrical Ballads* can be read as a broader anthropologic engagement with imperialism and colonialism. For Bewell, the volume asks what it means to be human, integrating American Indians, travelling pedlars and female vagrants into a poetry of common life that serves to erase the differences by which slavery had previously been justified.[14] The revolutions in America and France had focused attention on the rights of many previously disenfranchised groups, and a reinforced respect for human liberty and rights laid the foundations for the development of the Victorian liberal state.

Wordsworth was appalled, then, when the British government seemed to renege on this commitment to human liberty during the events surrounding France's invasion of Spain in 1808 under Napoleon. In an effort to defend Spain, Britain defeated the French army, but then failed to punish them for their actions. This concerned Wordsworth not simply because Britain appeared to be tolerating French tyranny, but also because it exhibited disrespect to the Spanish and Portuguese people. In *The Convention of Cintra* (1809), Wordsworth argued that their revolutionary spirit had been driven by a freedom rooted in both the imagination and religious faith, voicing as it did a collective politics free of gagging acts and military containment, and promoting the rights of the people to speak and be heard.

Some modern critics, like the literary historian James Chandler, hear a conservative and loyalist motive in Wordsworth's argument. Chandler suggests that Wordsworth's investment in the experience and feelings of real people, rather than the abstract theories of Enlightenment, aligns him with the conservative Edmund Burke.[15] Yet Wordsworth was much closer to Fox's Whig politics than to the Tory position, and urged the British government to endorse freedom of speech, abroad and at home, as 'an indispensable condition of all civil liberty' (*PW*, I.285). Spain and Portugal were motivated to throw off the autocratic rule of both their old governments and new dictators, he declared, by a belief in 'the moral virtues and qualities of passion which belong to a people', a claim which would have horrified Burke (*PW*, I.235).

Wordsworth regarded this 'passion' of the Spanish and Portuguese equivalent to the domestic affections once found amongst the labouring classes in Britain, one that unified communities while allowing for individual experience of this shared feeling. 'The outermost and all-embracing circle of benevolence has inward concentric circles', he wrote, 'which, like those of the spider's web, are bound together by links, and rest upon each other; making one frame, and capable of one tremor; circles narrower and narrower, closer and closer, as they lie more near to the centre of self from which they proceeded, and which sustains the whole' (*PW*, I.340). This web imagery is useful because it captures Wordsworth's sense of community as one bound in both strength and vulnerability: those who commit most fully to the group gain the most sustenance for themselves and others. Wordsworth might have shared a preference for experience over abstraction with Burke, then, but it was an emotional form of experience that he valued, one charged by religious as well as patriotic feeling, and made sense of through an imaginative power based on opposition to human oppression.

Community

At the end of *The Convention of Cintra*, Wordsworth describes his model community as 'spiritual', one that binds 'together the living and the dead' (*PW*, I.339). He used this phrase in *The Prelude* too, describing the community that saved him from his disillusionment after the failure of the French Revolution as comprising 'The noble Living and the noble Dead' (*P*, X.969). For Wordsworth, the dead are equal to the living because they, perhaps even more than those with whom we interact every day, have the power to summon up feeling within us. Our affection for the dead, Wordsworth insists, is healing and redemptive. Those detached from their capacity to feel, by circumstance or depression, are reintegrated into community and potentially restored to emotional health by being aware of others. If engaging with the living proves too overwhelming, the dead can offer solace.

The idea of 'community' always involves thinking about others for Wordsworth, and so, for him, represents an imaginative process: by having compassion for others, we are able to perceive the world around us through domestic affection rather than material gain. Once freed from an obsession with the objects of material life the individual can focus on human relations, so creating the conditions for shared love between groups of people that might not otherwise connect. The poet's own domestic life was representative of this all-encompassing model of community: the Wordsworth household, wherever it was geographically located, was held together by Dorothy, Mary and Sara, but regularly accommodated Coleridge and his children, Charles Lamb, Thomas De Quincey, numerous Hutchinsons and anyone else visiting that week.

This inclusive familial framework was affective and sentimental, sustained by emotion rather than inheritance alone. The eighteenth-century promotion of 'sensibility' – refined feeling associated with virtue and sensitivity – was similarly democratizing: everyone, it was conjectured, could feel. This belief was one source of the explosive conversion rates achieved by the Methodist preacher, John Wesley, who advocated a 'religion of the heart' that offered believers the chance to approach God through personal emotion. Under the banner of religious sensibility, Wesley vociferously opposed immoral pursuits such as cock-fighting and bear-baiting, as well as the potentially indecorous pleasure centres of the tavern and coffeehouse. For Wesley, human nature was not debauched and selfish, but instinctively compassionate and kind.

Wesley was also one of few public figures who translated these 'feminine' virtues into material change for women, advocating female preachers and declaring that 'there is no difference' between men and women before God. 'You, as well as men, are rational creatures', Wesley wrote to his female converts, 'You, like them, were made in the image of God; you are equally candidates for immortality; you too are called of God.'[16] For Hannah More, writing in 1799, women were also more attuned to justice and righteousness than men, possessing 'a tact which often enables them to feel what is just more instantaneously than they can define it'.[17] Even so, while women excelled as writers in this period, for most intellectuals the ideal thinker remained, as Coleridge wrote, a man with a male mind and female soul.[18]

Wordsworth, however, thought differently. His turn to Dorothy at the end of 'Tintern Abbey' (1798) can be read in relation to feminized sensibility, the poet pronouncing his sister the source of 'quietness and beauty' that sustains his 'chearful faith' against the 'dreary intercourse of daily life' (128–34). But Dorothy was never simply a feminine presence in Wordsworth's life, being instead a woman to whom he endlessly, and very publicly, confessed his poetic and emotional debt: 'She gave me eyes, she gave me ears; / And humble cares, and delicate fears; / A heart, the fountain of sweet tears; / And love, and thought, and joy' (17–20), he wrote in 'The Sparrow's Nest' (1802). These lines show us that Wordsworth had mixed feelings about sensibility: he accepted its sanction of feeling as central to life; but also rejected it as a fashionable and insincere ideology of feeling unable to integrate real feelings of love and joy. So while sensibility located feeling as central to life, and also to literature, it also threatened to artificially regulate feeling as something to be learned rather than participated in.

Modern criticism struggles with the idea of genuinely experiencing 'authentic' feeling, insisting as it does that all interpretation is ideologically mediated. Wordsworth shows us, however, that while the experience of feeling is always arbitrated by individual circumstances and the time and place of its occurrence, it remains personal and particular to the individual. To describe it otherwise only alienates people from their own histories and lives. His poetry thus teaches us how to feel, while at the same time offering an example of how one individual – William Wordsworth – sought to articulate, describe and sometimes liberate himself from his own good and bad feelings. He wished to evoke emotional responses in his readers, not to engender a closed debate about feeling, but to focus them on what it means to be human – to keep the 'Reader in the company of flesh and blood' (*PW*, I.130).

The poet John Keats' belief that 'Wordsworth is deeper than Milton' is founded on his sense that Wordsworth's poetry takes readers into the 'dark passages' of feeling, 'Misery and Heartbreak, Pain, Sickness and oppression', and then safely leads them out again.[19] Wordsworth's poetry overflows with feeling, not to gush and flood readers, but to keep feelings in circulation within an enclosed linguistic unit (the poem's form), enabling them to experience such things thoughtfully and over time. As Wordsworth claimed in *The Prelude*, his poetic project was committed to assessing to what extent 'words can give, / A substance and a life to what I feel', allowing him to examine and then accept his own feelings of loss, abandonment, grief and loneliness as well as joy, affection and repose (*P*, XI.340–1).

He also recognized that talking about feelings often blocks the experience of them, and used his poetry to address his private feelings (the only ones to which he had access) in order to create the conditions for his readers to contemplate their own. Moreover, Wordsworth speaks most directly to those who are uncomfortable with the potential intensity that emotions evoke. Many of his early poems, 'Nutting' (1798) and 'Michael', for example, embed and displace feeling only to reveal that this very repression is an (albeit unhealthy) form of emotional expression. Wordsworth's most thoughtful modern critic, Geoffrey Hartman, notes that Wordsworth's poetry 'absorbs' difficult thoughts and feelings, drawing readers in by evoking an emotional response that joins them with the poet in a kind of collective emotion or community of feeling.[20] This community is not abstract and theoretical, but presents a model of togetherness free of unresolved emotional tension. Communal feeling, Wordsworth thought, was imperative to a society damaged by the impact of war, industrialization and capitalism, especially one that looked to, even if it was not reliant upon, an experience of the transcendent.

Religion

While a majority in Britain retained an investment in God as the main source of transcendence and spiritual fulfilment, others turned to poetry as a substitute for faith. Many readers regarded Wordsworth as a 'spiritual counsellor', especially the Victorians, who were eager to align his poetry with various forms of belief system. Yet by the 1840s Wordsworth insisted that he had always 'been averse to frequent mention of the mysteries of Christian faith'; on first acquaintance, Coleridge had considered his new friend 'at least a *Semi*-atheist'.[21] Certainly Wordsworth's own religious commitments were various and shifting, rooted in schoolboy knowledge of the Bible, and developed through a mature nature-vision whereby God is merged into objects in the natural world.

Nature was 'propaedeutic' for Wordsworth, which meant it served as a sacrosanct teacher who prepared him both for a sustained contemplation of his environment, and for the assessment of deeper religious questions. These questions only took on significance for Wordsworth, however, when they enabled him to reflect back on his emotional responses to the world, material and immaterial alike. This approach was rooted in an eighteenth-century investment in religious emotion. The believer related to God through feeling either in an openly demonstrative manner (as in the case of Methodism and Evangelicalism), through socially responsible benevolence (associated with the Quakers and Unitarians), or through reserved and mystical forms of worship (favoured by Tractarianism and Roman Catholicism). Just as the landscape mattered to Wordsworth but had greater significance as a cognitive trigger to energize his imagination, so religion offered him a language of suffering, redemption and love that allowed him to write poetry. As he wrote in *The Prelude*, religion embodied a 'Visionary Power' that 'Attends upon the motions of the winds / Embodied in the mystery of words' (*P*, V.619–21).

As with so many of Wordsworth's views on subjects important to him, however, his religious opinions can seem inconsistent and abstract. He found the Bible an immense 'storehouse' (*PW*, III.34) of poetic images, but rarely quotes directly from it. He was appalled by religious intolerance, especially to members of the Jewish community, but was ambivalent about dissenters and despised Roman Catholicism. These contradictions have allowed believers from all faiths to claim his poetry as reflective of their own systems, especially the High Church group known as the Oxford Movement. Before turning to the poet's connections with this movement, however, we need to briefly map out the religious landscape with which Wordsworth engaged.

The Church of England dominated religious politics in eighteenth- and nineteenth-century Britain, and is synonymous with Anglicanism. It enforced civil and national allegiance by excluding from public office individuals not prepared to follow its set of doctrinal statements, the 'Thirty-nine Articles', established in 1563. The Act of Toleration (1689) granted limited rights back to those dissenters who felt unable to agree with these doctrines, but they, like Roman Catholics and Jews, had to wait until the nineteenth century to secure equal rights with Anglicans in Britain. Dissenters found Anglicanism problematic in part because of its reliance on practices that they saw as a distraction from the Bible. For them, the Bible was the only resource Christians needed to practise their faith, and they chose to discuss and study scripture, not in churches and cathedrals, but in local chapels. Within the chapel, dissenters sought to present Christianity as a compassionate and ethical movement, favouring an effusive and emotional form of public prayer.

Dissent did not comprise a unified group of believers, however. 'Old Dissent' was invested in re-emotionalizing Christian belief, and arguing that the individual could reach God through reason (intellectual knowledge) and faith (affective knowledge). Such believers included Presbyterians, Protestants for whom the Church is administered through a group of elected members; and Quakers, or the Society of Friends, who argued that religious truth was received through the inner voice of God speaking directly to the soul, and not via ordained ministers. The Quakers in particular seemed close to the Romantics in their approach to God, valuing simplicity of feeling and the emotional experience of faith. 'New Dissent' included reformed Presbyterians and Unitarians. The most prominent were Unitarians, believers who held that God was a single, intelligent and wise power whose being comprises all time and space; a belief that everything is an attribute of God, however, denied Christ's unique divinity. Unitarianism thus signified as an openly radical religion by the end of the eighteenth century; Coleridge even worked as a Unitarian lay preacher in the 1790s. Like many new dissenters, however, Coleridge also began to find Unitarianism excessively rational and dry, a 'secular' religion that squeezed out the sacred and experiential aspects of faith.

While Coleridge turned back to Anglicanism, large numbers of believers had been drawn into the Evangelical Revival, a movement that was anything but rational and dry. Unlike dissenters, Evangelicals argued that their mission was compatible with the orthodoxy represented by the Church of England. They sought to reintroduce into the Church the mystical and supernatural elements of religion which dissent had attempted to render redundant. Evangelicals also encouraged believers to enthusiastically effuse their love of God in church and in public, and invested heavily in the idea of personal faith. The most successful aspect of the Evangelical Revival had been John and Charles Wesley's Methodist movement, which converted over half a million people in Britain between 1740 and 1840. A 'religion of the heart', Methodism valued the believer's affective and personal relationship with God. Never a Methodist himself, Wordsworth diverted his own interest in the relationship between the individual and God into 'pantheism'. Proclaiming God's immanence in nature, pantheism underlines Wordsworth's description of God in 'Tintern Abbey', a presence or power 'deeply interfused' in the 'setting suns, / And the round ocean, and the living air, /And the blue sky, and in the mind of man' (97–100).

Wordsworth's late work too shows how he continued to respect and revere the specificity and mystery of nature. From the 1830s, however, followers of the so-called Oxford Movement or 'Tractarians' would claim Wordsworth's poetry for themselves. If dissenters thought the Church of England too orthodox, the Oxford Movement thought it not orthodox enough. Its proponents worked to spiritualize the Church of England by re-establishing medieval liturgical practices, like burning incense in church, and also hierarchical order, by upholding the idea of 'Apostolic Succession' (the Roman Catholic idea that spiritual authority had been passed down from the Apostles through successive bishops and popes). Tractarianism also stressed the ceremonial and emotional aspects of faith, and one of its chief advocates, the former Evangelical and poet, John Henry Newman, described it as 'not so much a movement as a "spirit afloat", it was within us, "rising up in hearts"'.[22] The problem for many Anglicans, including Wordsworth, was that such a spirit seemed anchored in Roman Catholicism, a religion that threatened the British constitution through its allegiance to a pope rather than to a monarch.

For the Oxford Movement, however, ideas and doctrines that sounded Catholic (confession, monasteries, sisterhoods and the eucharist – the Christian ceremony celebrating the Last Supper) were actually central to the Church of England. Promoting an elevated and ceremonial form of worship, Oxford Movement supporters like Newman and Frederick Faber argued that Wordsworth's poetry seemed ideally to realize their faith's experiential inclinations. Faber, who was also the acting curate of Ambleside and tutor to Wordsworth's cousin, Dorothy Harrison, was insistent that Wordsworth was the laureate of High Church sensibility, a claim echoed by John Keble. Having venerated Wordsworth as the laureate of the poor, during the ceremony marking Wordsworth's honorary doctorate from Oxford, Keble also dedicated his *Lectures on*

Poetry (1832–41) to him as the 'chief minister' of 'sweetest poetry' and 'of high and sacred truth'.[23]

Wordsworth was ambivalent about his association with the Oxford Movement. On the one hand, he had insisted as early as 1812 that he would shed his own blood defending the Church of England from the 'terror' of Roman Catholicism. Wordsworth's vehement opposition to the Catholic Emancipation Act (1829) was characteristic of a general and widespread fear that the Catholics would continue to see the Pope as their real authority, not the royal personage. On the other hand, he responded to overtures made by individuals who saw in him a national poet defending Britain's spiritual inheritance. Tractarian poetry was one of the most successful literary events in history, Keble's *The Christian Year*, for example, annually selling over 10,000 volumes for at least fifty years after its publication in 1827. Keble's description of 'poetry as a vent for overcharged feelings' in his *Lectures on Poetry*, forwarding poetry as the best route to the divine, echoed one of Wordsworth's own poetic theories. For Keble, poetry 'is the indirect expression in words, most appropriately in metrical words, of some overpowering emotion, or ruling taste, or feeling, the direct indulgence whereof is somehow repressed'.[24] The next chapter will contextualize this notion of poetry as an emotive and oblique genre, with reference to Wordsworth's commentaries on poetic form and poetic theory.

Poetics

Wordsworth thought a lot about how and why he wrote poetry. These ideas, or his poetics, centre on the notion that our entire experience and perception of the world is shaped through the medium of words, little units of meaning that have the power to modify and change the way we see and understand. Words take on even more significance for him when located within a poem: they are transfigured by different kinds of form, metre and rhythm that recast their meaning through sounds and patterns. He spent considerable time selecting each word that appears in his poetry, claiming to compose his verse and prose with the 'slow and laborious hand' of the memorial mason (*PW*, II.60). Words, Wordsworth stated, are 'too awful an instrument for good and evil to be trifled with', 'an incarnation' of our thoughts serving to give them meaning and vitality. Once language is used 'only as a clothing' for meaning, he argued, it becomes a 'counter-spirit' to understanding, dissolving our experience of life into abstraction (*PW*, II.85).

Wordsworth was concerned that his eighteenth-century predecessors, as well as many of his peers, had become locked into a dead and spiritless poetic language, employing only 'mechanical' and artificial words to write about 'feelings and ideas with which they had no natural connection whatsoever' (*PW*, I.131, 160). Their poetry seemed to him excessively stylized and fake, articulating ideas that were flamboyant or entertaining rather than authentic and real. Confronted by the 'distorted language' this poetry used, he argued, readers are cast into a 'perturbed and unusual state of mind'. This in turn blocks them from the experience of 'pleasure' that poetry ought to produce: a condition of being or mindfulness that is at once composed and animated (*PW*, I.160). In reaction against the elevated diction of eighteenth-century poetry, then, Wordsworth sought to metrically arrange 'the real language of men in a state of vivid sensation' in order to summon the actual everyday thoughts and feelings human beings experience (*PW*, I.118).

The following discussion explores Wordsworth's use of 'real language' to suggest that his choice of words – his poetic diction – offers us a portal on to what he considered the purpose of poetry: to enable readers to experience a 'powerful feeling' that grants insight into and a compassionate engagement with one's community and environment. By gripping, even shocking, the reader with his depictions of strange rustic scenes and people, he invites us to think about the way we hear, see and feel these images and then reflect on the particular interpretive biases, interests and methodologies of that reading experience. As Wordsworth argued, 'descriptions, either of passions, manners, or characters' are 'read a hundred times' in verse, where 'prose is read once', poetry encouraging repeated readings that magnify the emotional experience presented (*PW*, I.150).

We also tend to read poetry more than once so that we can explore the way it plays with rhythms and sounds, an aspect of poetics called prosody. Wordsworth suggests that poetry conveys our experience of life in even more vivid and animating terms than prose because the poetic arrangement of words into various forms, rhythms and metres creates an extra layer of meaning. Metre can both regulate the poetic voice by managing the 'spontaneous overflow of feelings' poetry evokes in the reader (*PW*, I.126); but it can also destabilize this voice, offering up oblique and implied meanings variously dependent on speech patterns, accents and dialects. The rhythm of a poem not only differs from reader to reader, but also changes as the individual reads and rereads it, sometimes stressing one word sometimes another, and so exemplifying Wordsworth's understanding of poetry as a site of interplay between meanings, rhythms and language. This is why Wordsworth's poetry is understood to signify through the reader's emotional response to it, 'the feeling therein developed' giving 'importance to the action and situation, and not the action and situation to the feeling' (*PW*, I.128). It is the feeling we are left with after reading one of Wordsworth's poems that helps us to interpret what we have read by guiding us back to those particular words and phrases that we most remember.

This chapter first explores the kinds of words and metres Wordsworth considers most effective in evoking our feelings; and second, outlines the poetic forms he most commonly employs: blank verse, the sonnet, the ode, elegy and epitaph. Readers unfamiliar with prosodic debates should bear in mind that however committed Wordsworth was to metrical rule, he always advocated the 'spirit of the versification' over the 'letter of the metre', encouraging us to think and feel 'the music of the poem' for ourselves (*PW*, III.29–30). His most famous collection, the *Lyrical Ballads*, is itself made up of a hybrid form, comprised of the first-person lyric (a traditionally non-narrative form associated with the direct expression of emotions) and the ballad (a strongly narrative form marked by repeated rhymes to keep the story moving). This willingness to experiment with poetry suggests that Wordsworth is invested in imaginatively playing with form, and encouraged his reader to do the same. As he declared in the 'Preface' (1802) to this collection: 'I have one request to make of my Reader, which is, that in judging these Poems he would decide by his own feelings genuinely, and not by reflection upon what will probably be the judgment of others' (*PW*, I.155).

Poetic diction

For Wordsworth, poetic diction comprises two elements: language (the words he uses to write poems) and metre (the rhythms and sound patterns he creates by using words in particular ways). In the 'Advertisement' (1798) and expanded 'Preface' (1800; 1802) to the *Lyrical Ballads*, he argues that his main concern is to mould everyday language into metrical forms, that is, to versify 'human passions, human characters, and human incidents' in the 'real language of men' (*PW*, I.116). Readers disagree on how unique this project was: the critic Marilyn Butler, for example, suggests that Wordsworth's poetic experiments were already current in popular eighteenth-century magazine poetry and so are relatively unexceptional.[1] The Romantic writer William Hazlitt, however, argued that the *Lyrical Ballads* were both politically challenging and more difficult than popular verse. He claimed that while the 'trifling' subject matter of the poems might not have been unusual, the 'profound' and weighty 'reflections' they provoked offered intellectual and emotional acuity into the nature of the self, consciousness and the imagination.[2]

Wordsworth's key innovation, however, was that he sought to lay bare the ideological underpinnings of both the words commonly chosen to describe 'incidents and situations from common life', and also the way readers respond to them (*PW*, I.123). The rustic and uncultured feel of the *Lyrical Ballads*, for example, derives not from long descriptions of rural life, but instead from the use of simple repeated words and phrases that capture the recurring routines, as well as harsh conditions, that characterize lower-class life and labour. The poet knows that his middle-class readers are accustomed to complacently, if sentimentally, reacting to the ballad form: these readers assume that the correct response to a lyrical ballad such as 'Simon Lee, the Old Huntsman' (1798), for example, is one of pity, compassion and kindness coupled with a desire to resolve or fix his situation. The undecorated language and metre Wordsworth uses to depict the displaced, aged and sick Simon Lee in fact challenges these readers to reflect on their understanding of the poem. By presenting Lee's story so starkly, Wordsworth overturns easy and predictable hypotheses about the labouring classes and forces readers to question the agenda behind their emotional response and the political conditions that have given rise to the poem's scenario.

Wordsworth's insistence that the reader morally respond to his work, however, can prove disquieting. His correspondence with a young admirer called John Wilson underlines this, one in which they discuss the lyrical ballad 'The Idiot Boy' (1798), in which a mentally ill child is sent to fetch a doctor for a sick neighbour. When the child gets lost, his mother goes in search of him, as does the neighbour whose concern for her friend's son has distracted her from her illness. Wilson told Wordsworth that he had felt considerable distress after reading the poem. The poet replied that this was exactly the reaction he had wanted, the poem written to induce discomfort and urge readers to face up to their 'disgusted' reactions to the 'unsightly and unsmooth' aspects of existence. The poet declares that he deliberately used the word 'idiot' (rather than more humorous terms like 'lack-wit, half-wit, witless, etc.') to realize this edgy reading experience. For Wordsworth, it isn't enough for a poet to describe feelings his readers would 'sympathise with': the poet should also write about uncomfortable scenarios, which his readers would be 'better and more moral beings if they did sympathise with.'[3]

His poems attempt to achieve this by first, emotionally arresting the reader by using a raw and 'naked' language and form; second, drawing attention to the ideological motivations of our emotional reaction; and third, encouraging us to reflect on this reaction within the hypnotic sound of the poem's rhythms. In 'The Idiot Boy', we are riveted and unsettled by the story, but simultaneously introduced to 'new compositions of feeling' in the poem that evoke the daily experiences of people unable to ignore the rawer elements of life because they cannot afford to do so (Betty Foy is financially, as well as emotionally, prevented from shutting her son away in an asylum). Rural community is thus held together by what the poet perceived to be a 'strength, disinterestedness, and grandeur of love' that he attempts to invoke in his poetry to neutralize, or flood 'like a deluge', the 'feeble sensation of disgust and aversion' men like Wilson might initially feel on reading the poem.

Wordsworth sought to find a language that granted pleasure to his reader, then, not by superficially delighting them, but by stimulating feelings of compassion and duty. His poems, he wrote, each have 'a worthy purpose' (*PW*, I.124). He related 'incidents and situations from common life' in 'an unusual way' to counter 'urbanite affectations of eighteenth-century poesy', cheap 'frantic novels' and 'extravagant stories in verse': all of these genres, he thought, corroded readers' capacity to meditate on the 'repeated experience and regular feelings' of the lower classes (*PW*, I.123, 128, 124). Such meditation was important because it encouraged readers to reflect on 'the essential passions of the heart' (*PW*, I.124) in a process that made them think and feel about real, rather than abstract, situations. 'The Idiot Boy' and a further lyrical ballad called 'The Mad Mother' (1798), for example, do not seek to define a generalized notion of 'maternal passion', but instead provoke the reader into experiencing the particular maternal struggles both poems embody (*PW*, I.126).

One accusation sometimes levelled at Wordsworth's intentionally sympathy-inducing style, however, is that it might fabricate feeling, rather than genuinely invoke it. The poet attempted to remedy this tension by highlighting metre as that which constantly overturns and so renews our emotional response as we go along. Verse, from the Latin *versus* or 'turning', is suggestive of the way Wordsworth turns or transforms what he sees into words and then into experiences and feelings, an argument he outlines in his 1802 revision of the 1800 'Preface' to the *Lyrical Ballads*. In the 1802 'Preface', Wordsworth maintains that metre enables readers to confront painful topics in a way prose does not, divesting language 'of its reality' by throwing 'a sort of half consciousness of unsubstantial existence over the whole composition' (*PW*, I.147). Metre temporarily de-realizes the world to make the reader work to bring it back into focus and discover its 'truth' – not a truth that explains or fixes what is really going on in the poem – but one that gives us access to a sense of what the poem means in the moment in which we read it. This truth has nothing to do with 'external testimony', Wordsworth writes, but is instead 'carried alive into the heart by passion', made real through the reader's feeling (*PW*, I.139). This kind of reading experience allows us to see imaginatively, finding meaning in all aspects of life, especially those that seem trivial or inconsequential.

Strict metres in particular enable this reading experience because they impress repeated thoughts and feelings into our bodies and memories. Dorothy, for example, experienced a strong feeling of solace by reciting over and over two lines from Wordsworth's poem 'The Solitary Reaper': 'O listen! for the Vale profound / Is overflowing with the sound' (7–8). She described this feeling as 'inexpressibly soothing', repeating the lines to herself 'in disconnection with any thought' simply to call up their gentle sound.[4] The Victorian aesthete Walter Pater also argued that Wordsworth's ability to fuse compelling but simple words with metre created a 'rhythmical power' with the capacity to act as a kind of 'sedative' that at once arouses and regulates our emotional response to the poem.[5] As Wordsworth argued, the 'regular and uniform' presence of metre in poetry has 'great efficacy in tempering and restraining the passion by an intertexture of ordinary feeling', the reader's excited feelings checked by underlying, habitual ones (*PW*, I.146). The reader hears 'real' language, then, but it is 'fitted' by metrical arrangement into the poem's frame in a process that 'divest[s]' this language of its reality to make it temporarily strange and so give us new insights into our own readings (*PW*, I.139, 147).

In the lyrical ballad 'Goody Blake and Harry Gill' (1798), for example, we are presented with a scene of common life communicated by the familiar beat of the ballad metre. Yet the fact this stable metre carries along an almost supernatural story about a landowner's metamorphosis from a 'lusty drover' into a freezing and skeletal spectre also unsettles us. Wordsworth's point is that from the ordinary and everyday spring the most shocking and impassioned moments, and we can only make sense of them by thinking carefully through them in a state of 'tranquillity' (*PW*, I.149). The task of the poet is to teach us how to recollect emotion in tranquillity as a figure with an unusual capacity to conjure 'up in himself passions' and 'a greater readiness and power in expressing what he thinks and feels' (*PW*, I.138). The poet is not superior to others (Wordsworth rejects the role of transcendent seer in the 'Preface'), but 'thinks and feels in the spirit of the passions of men' in a more pronounced manner in order to offer an example of the feeling individual. The poet is freed to acknowledge the 'beauty of the universe' because he truly respects what he sees, committed as he is to looking 'at the world in the spirit of love' (*PW*, I.142, 140). Later Romantic poets may have approved Percy Bysshe Shelley's idea that the poet is a 'nightingale, who sits in darkness and sings to cheer its own solitude'; but for Wordsworth, the poet is someone able to sing 'a song in which all human beings join with him' (*PW*, I.141).[6]

Blank verse

Wordsworth is perhaps most well known for his use of blank verse, significantly in *The Prelude*. Many readers overlook his commitment to this form, however, partly because critics treat his blank verse as if it spontaneously poured from him as he wandered through the countryside. Dorothy's *Grasmere Journals*, however, suggest that Wordsworth's habits of composition involved a close interplay between walking in the natural world, conversing with others and physical acts of writing. As she recalls: 'After William rose we went & sate in the orchard till dinner time. We walked a long time in the Evening upon our favourite path – the owls hooted, the night-hawk sang to itself' and 'I left William writing a few lines about the night-hawk and other images of the evening, & went to seek for letters – none were come. – We walked backwards & forwards a little, after I returned to William.'[7]

Dorothy highlights the communal and contemplative aspect of Wordsworth's writing process here, suggesting its intimate connection to his walking habits. We hear a similar idea related by one of the gardeners at Rydal Mount, who vividly remembered Wordsworth's routine of composing, writing and walking:

> he would set his heäd a bit forrad, and put his hands behint his back. And then he would start bumming, and it was bum, bum, bum, stop; then bum, bum, bum, reet down till t'other end, and then he'd set down and git a bit o' paper out and write a bit; and then he git up, and bum, bum, bum, and goa on bumming for long enough right down and back agean.[8]

This account of Wordsworth's writing process suggests that it was a gradual and laboured one: the poet regularly suffered from headaches, exhaustion, chest, bowel and eye complaints before and during periods of intense composition. Yet the gardener's reminiscence also hints at the manner in which Wordsworth felt his way into blank verse metre, the 'bum, bum, bum' of his walk recalling the de-dum, de-dum, de-dum rhythm of blank-verse iambic pentameter. Certainly blank verse was far from spontaneous or effortless for Wordsworth – he described it as 'infinitely the most difficult metre to manage' – but he succeeds in it by embodying the rhythm (in his walking) and then transcribing it through language as poetry.[9]

Wordsworth was drawn to blank verse for two significant, and connected, reasons: first, it was regarded as a politically radical form; and second, it was associated with John Milton. Blank verse connoted reformism because its metre granted the poet rhythmic space to play with words, liberating him or her from what Milton called 'the modern bondage of rhyming'.[10] The poet was still expected to employ the five-beat iambic pentameter line, but blank verse nevertheless allowed for hypermetrical lines (where a line contains more than ten syllables and so 'goes over' five beats). The formalist critic Simon Jarvis points out that Wordsworth often writes hypermetrically when he loses control over language because of some emotional or intellectual 'pressure' that causes him to blurt out phrases or words that unsettle the metre.[11] The steady iambic pentameter of 'There was a Boy' (1798), for example, is disturbed instantly by a series of caesural or 'medial' pauses in the first two lines that alert readers to the troubled content of the poem: 'There was a Boy, ye knew him well, ye Cliffs / And Islands of Winander!' (1–2). The commas and exclamation mark break up the rhythm here to allow readers to shift their emotional state in accordance with the poem's elegiac tone.

For Wordsworth, then, blank verse offered a steady rhythm inside which he could experiment with metre, pauses and the emotional response of his readers. While Coleridge suggested that blank verse was 'metre to the eye only', Wordsworth argued that it actually slowed down the reading process, inviting readers to stress the final syllables of each line and then pause, so bringing out the 'passion' of the poem's subject and sound alike.[12] Wordsworth thus used the form in poems that normally would have been written as ballads or lyrics. He started his poem 'Michael', for example, as a pastoral ballad, a form traditionally suited to its narrative about the demise of a shepherd and his family after they lose their inherited land due to enclosure. Yet after living with the poem's narrative for a while, Wordsworth decided that the shepherd's tale deserved to be voiced through the contemplative and unhurried measures of blank verse. This change of mind deeply upset some readers: the politician Charles James Fox even claimed that stories about shepherds did not warrant the same metrical form as great poems like *Paradise Lost*. Wordsworth, by contrast, claimed that the depth of feeling and passion inherent in everyday rural life gave it precisely the same claim to blank verse as Milton's famous epic poem.

Wordsworth consequently wrote a lot of blank verse, composing over 5,000 lines of it between 1796 and 1800, including early drafts of *The Prelude*, *The Borderers* and 'The Ruined Cottage'. He commonly uses the standard decasyllabic line (a line with ten syllables) in his blank verse, but then deliberately breaks the pattern if the regularity of the beat threatens to overwhelm the emotional content of the poem. In 'The Brothers', for example, Wordsworth frequently adds unstressed 'extra' syllables to the ends of lines to make the poem sound more conversational ('Poor Walter! whether it was care that spurred him', 214). In the more reflective 'Tintern Abbey', however, Wordsworth tends to stress the third, usually offbeat syllable, to disrupt the metre and slow it down. This effect is exemplified by the emphasis on 'sad' in 'The still, *sad* music of humanity' (92). This line illustrates one of Wordsworth's frequent blank-verse techniques: he begins by using an unhurried pace ('The still, *sad*') but then closes the line with a speedy ending ('music of humanity'). He also uses another trademark technique in 'Tintern Abbey' called syntactic inversion, meaning reversed word orders ('Therefore am I still / A lover of the meadows', 103–4); and enjambment, sentences that continue over two or more lines ('I cannot paint / What then I was', 75–6). In contrast to the syntactically contained lines of 'Michael', the run-on lines of 'Tintern Abbey' are suggestive of a mind in deep thought, unable to compartmentalize the complexities being pondered, but rescued from its cognitive maze by the invisible force of line endings.[13]

If 'Tintern Abbey' is steeped in a blank verse of enjambment and mid-line pauses to convey the meditative emotions of the narrator, 'A Night-Piece' (1798) uses an impulsive and fluctuating metre to depict a more startled and disturbed set of feelings. The poem – which Wordsworth considered his best example of blank verse – captures the sensation of astonishment the narrator sustains on encountering the sudden illumination of the sky by the moon and stars as they appear from behind an obscuring cloud. Readers are invited into the narrator's vision and consequent awe as 'the clouds are split / Asunder, – and above his head he sees / The clear Moon, and the glory of the heavens' by a string of offbeats and double offbeats, starker still against the neutral and regular metre at the poem's beginning and close. Employing volatile and regular metres in the same poem allows Wordsworth to present overwhelming, painful or frightening experiences even as he offers readers a way to think about them through steady reflection.

Sonnets

Wordsworth's use of blank verse to invoke reflection is taken in part from his reading of Milton's verse, of which he knew hundreds of lines by heart. The poet makes countless, and often unconscious, metrical allusions to *Paradise Lost* in *The Prelude*, but he was also deeply affected by Milton's sonnets. He told his friend Isabella Fenwick that his particular awakening to them occurred 'in the cottage of Town-End, one afternoon, in 1801', whereupon 'my Sister read to me the Sonnets of Milton. I had long been well acquainted with them, but I was particularly struck on that occasion with the dignified simplicity and majestic harmony that runs through most of them – in character so totally different from the Italian, and still more so from Shakespeare's fine Sonnets'.[14]

Milton's sonnets were generally recognized as 'the great model and archetype' of the form by the nineteenth century, and Wordsworth was eager to imitate their style. As a reviewer in *The Gentleman's Magazine* (1841) declared: 'We think Milton's the finest sonnets of the old days of poetry, and Wordsworth's of the present.'[15] Even Francis Jeffrey, usually so hostile to Wordsworth, was forced to admit Wordsworth's skill with the sonnet form: 'All English writers of sonnets have imitated Milton', he wrote, 'and, in this way, Mr Wordsworth, when he writes sonnets, escapes again from the trammels of his own unfortunate system; and the consequence is, that his sonnets are as much superior to the greater part of his other poems, as Milton's sonnets are superior to his.'[16]

Wordsworth appears to have taken Jeffrey's comment on board: he wrote over 500 sonnets and several sonnet series (the phrase 'sonnet sequence' is not current until later in the nineteenth century), including the *Sonnets Dedicated to Liberty* (1807), the *Ecclesiastical Sketches* (1822), *The River Duddon: A Series of Sonnets* (1820) and *Sonnets upon the Punishment of Death* (1841). This focus on the sonnet may at first seem incongruous with Wordsworth's commitment to the 'real language of men', the form a very stylized one that even the poet initially considered 'egregiously absurd'.[17] Yet Wordsworth eventually favoured the sonnet because of its potential as a closed space in which an intense emotional experience can be compacted, halted and then reflected on, granting the form a sense of unity other genres could not offer. By turning the sonnet into a snapshot of feeling, Wordsworth de-sentimentalized a form previously associated with sensibility by poets such as William Lisle Bowles, Charlotte Smith and Anna Seward. In 'Composed upon Westminster Bridge, September 3, 1803' (1807), for example, Wordsworth overlooks London not to effuse or gush about the city, but to transform it into a body of calm vitalized by a gently beating 'mighty heart' (14):

> Earth has not anything to shew more fair:
> Dull would he be of soul who could pass by
> A sight so touching in its majesty:
> This City now doth like a garment wear
> The beauty of the morning; silent, bare,
> Ships, towers, domes, theatres, and temples lie
> Open unto the fields, and to the sky;
> All bright and glittering in the smokeless air.
> Never did sun more beautifully steep
> In his first splendor valley, rock, or hill;
> Ne'er saw I, never felt, a calm so deep!
> The river glideth at his own sweet will:
> Dear God! the very houses seem asleep;
> And all that mighty heart is lying still!

The brevity of the poem's length and expression allows Wordsworth to use the sonnet as a way to summarize or condense moments of heightened consciousness, 'miniaturing' the world, as Coleridge put it 'in order to *manifest* the Truth'.[18] For Wordsworth, the sonnet form was like a fragile but harmonious piece of architecture, comprising an 'orbicular body, – a sphere – or a dewdrop'.[19]

The poet was intrigued by the idea of the sonnet as a perfectly formed space in which readers might feel calm and meditative. In his sonnet 'Nuns fret not at their convent's narrow room', Wordsworth suggests that the form functions like the spare and limited quarters in which nuns and hermits live. While their restricted environment is conducive to religious thoughts and prayer, the sonnet similarly focuses readers so that they too can enter into a state of deep contemplation and vision. The sonnet's unobtrusive structure also stops readers from turning their thoughts inward into excessive self-reflexivity. As a reviewer for the literary magazine, *The Athenaeum*, argued, the sonnet is 'well suited for pure thoughts and delicate fancies; but too calm, too restrained in its structure and progress, to afford a possible vehicle for the bursts, starts, throes, and outpourings of magnificent madness'.[20] The first fourteen lines of Wordsworth's sonnet, 'Old Man Travelling', for example, are structured like a blank-verse sonnet, moving from a description of the man's character and movement into a reflection on his apparent grace and patience. But when the reader discovers the man is going to visit his son in hospital, a victim of the violence of war, the poem breaks out of the sonnet form into a faltering and unsteady blank verse metre in order to capture the anxiety and sorrow inherent to the scene.

Wordsworth did not regard the sonnet as a passive or easily manipulated form, however, claiming for it a status as a literary and political facilitator. In 'Scorn not the Sonnet', for example, he suggests that the form granted William Shakespeare the 'Key' that 'unlocked his heart' (2–3) and enabled him to write, and gave the poets Petrarch and Tasso the 'small Lute' (4) and 'Pipe' (5) through which to voice their court music. At the same time, the sonnet is the stage on which Milton sounds his political 'Trumpet' (13), an image that renders the sonnet an explosive and even apocalyptic form. Wordsworth's Milton is one who can blow 'Soul-animating strains' (14) into the world like the angels in Revelation 8.2, so articulating a strong political commitment to liberty. Wordsworth also invokes Milton as the protector of this liberty and the saviour of England in the sonnet 'London, 1802', his poetic voice, 'whose sound was like the sea; / Pure as the naked heavens, majestic, free', able to guide the nation back to currently lost 'manners, virtue, freedom, power' (10–11, 8).

Wordsworth's construction of Milton as a Christ-like redeemer in his sonnets is also suggestive of the religious meaning the form held for him. His most obviously theological poems are the *Ecclesiastical Sketches* (1822), which inspired both Felicia Hemans' well-known sonnet series, 'Female Characters of Scripture' (1834) and also numerous sonnet collections issued by the Oxford Movement. Wordsworth's non-religious sonnets also enthused other writers, especially his 'tour sonnets' describing various trips he had ventured upon. His *Yarrow Revisited* (published in 1835), 'Poems Composed or Suggested during a Tour, in the Summer of 1833' and 'Memorials of a Tour in Italy, 1837' influenced John Bowring's 'Sonnets Written during a Late Tour in Italy', Aubrey de Vere's 'Atlantic Coast Scenery' and Catherine Godwin's 'Four Sonnets Written during a Summer Tour on the Continent'. The poet Charles Wyatt even wrote a sonnet addressed to a lady 'With a Volume of Wordsworth's Sonnets' (1837), confirming Wordsworth's place in what literary journals of the period soon called 'sonnettomania'.

It is unlikely, however, that Wyatt envisioned his lady reader with a copy of Wordsworth's 1841 series, *Sonnets upon the Punishment of Death* (1841). These odd sonnets present a case in support of the death penalty by arguing that the mere imprisonment of convicts only dehumanizes them by damning them to a life of sorrow or further crime. The sonnet form offered Wordsworth an ideal space for such disciplined thoughts. While a poetic defence of capital punishment might jar with Wordsworth's more gentle and meditative verse, one might argue that the deliberate choice of a form associated with wavering lovers and contradictory responses betrays the poet's awareness of the inconsistencies inherent to his polemic. His suggestion in sonnet IV, for example, that the abolition of the death penalty elevates death as 'the thing that ought / To be most dreaded' (5–6), is immediately countered in sonnet VIII, where state power is presented as more terrifying. On the other hand, Wordsworth's support for the death penalty in these sonnets might once more be traced to his devotion to Milton, who suggests in *Paradise Lost* that Adam and Eve are given a death sentence by God as a 'remedy' to their transgressions, releasing them from sin (*Paradise Lost*, XI.162).

Odes, elegies, epitaphs

Like all of Wordsworth's sonnets, his *Sonnets upon the Punishment of Death* invoke reflection on solemn themes. The idea of death obsessed Wordsworth, and his odes, elegies and epitaphs reveal different aspects of this fascination, portraying death as a refuge from life and the dead as intrinsic to living communities. Wordsworth claimed that his interest in death was rooted in his childhood, wherein he would brood over the relationship between the material and immaterial, life and death:

> Nothing was more difficult for me in my childhood than to admit the notion of death as a state applicable to my own being … I was often unable to think of external things as having external existence & I communed with all that I saw as something not apart from but inherent in my own immaterial nature. Many times while going to school have I grasped at a wall or tree to recall myself from this abyss of idealism to the reality.[21]

For Wordsworth, childhood permits an idealized vision of life that is gradually eroded by experience, the once 'dream-like vividness and splendour' of the world necessarily fading as we encounter bereavement, sorrow and injustice. Wordsworth used the elegy and ode to work through this shift from a state of credulity to disenchantment, both forms sharing a tone and style many eighteenth-century and Romantic poets considered appropriate for the expression of a visionary and imaginative poetics.

The elegy and ode also lend themselves to reflection on how we understand and relate to the passage of time, an uneasy subject that both forms help us to think about in their capacity to explore questions of eternity and transcendence. For Wordsworth both forms administer 'the comforts' of religion, while breathing the 'spirit of religion' into us, so granting access to questions of the unknown and infinite (*PW*, III.64). Poetry, more than any other genre, Wordsworth argued, was able to give expression to that religious 'wish of the human heart to supply in another state of existence the deficiencies of this'.[22] In other words, if life necessarily consists of a series of losses for Wordsworth – of innocence, faith, people, vision – the ode and the elegy offered him space to deal with his consequent bereaved feelings. In fact Wordsworth's preoccupation with grief and loss in his poetry renders nearly all of it potentially elegiac. The early deaths of his mother and father certainly haunt Wordsworth's poetry, as his narrators search for substitute guardians in nature and the divine. In doing so, Wordsworth strives to transform feelings of despair and sadness into joy by creating the conditions in which individuals might become conscious of and then accept their emotional state, and in doing so make peace with it.

The ode helps us make peace with upsetting experiences because of its consolatory content: ceremonial and panegyric (when written for public occasions); and meditative and philosophical (when composed for private reflection). English poetry tends to employ two specific kinds of ode: the Pindaric (characterized by two long, metrically identical stanzas – the strophe and antistrophe – followed by a shorter *epode* or 'turn' in a different metre); and the Horatian (a longer form with regular repeating stanzas). Romanticism created its own fragmented and vulnerable kind of ode called the effusion: Wordsworth's attempts include his 'Effusion in the Pleasure-Ground on the Banks of the Bran, near Dunkeld' (1814); and 'Extempore Effusion upon the Death of James Hogg' (1835).

Even Wordsworth's renowned 'Intimations Ode' (published in 1807) plays with the form's conventions, partly because it was written as a defence against critics like Coleridge who believed he had lost his poetic potential to experiment and innovate. The ode consequently maps Wordsworth's struggle with his own mortality and his realization that the once innocent and childlike perspective through which he viewed the world as an earthly heaven, 'Apparelled in celestial light' (4), is fragile and transitory. The most recognized trope in the 'Intimations Ode' is Wordsworth's fading 'visionary gleam' (56), an image in which he admits that his poetic light has seemingly begun to dim. As Wordsworth is plunged into a reflection on the loss of this 'gleam', the narrative voice shifts from the first to the second person to invite readers to think about their own 'shadowy recollections' (152) of grief and loss. Seen through these shadows, even nature – a field, a tree, a single flower – begins to feel like a 'prison-house' (67), its 'glory' (18) stripped away as it locks human experience into a process of organic decline.

With this decline, however, comes an acknowledgement that loss and suffering are as much part of the experience of life as joy and wonder, granting a kind of wholeness to subjectivity that allows for a new faith to emerge, one rooted in those feelings engendered by self-reflection and self-awareness. The ability to have these feelings thus allows the individual to think in such a way that goes beyond feeling. This is why the little flower that symbolizes atrophy and grief in line 54 is, by the end of the poem, able to 'give / Thoughts that do often lie too deep for tears' (205–6).

If the 'Intimations Ode' helped Wordsworth to redress his fears of death and transience through bringing together emotional insight with reflection, then his elegies offered a space to mourn specific deaths and become reconciled with intense feelings of loss and confusion. Elegy, a form in which the narrator mourns a death or other loss, is a discursive or meditative reflection that addresses pastoral, mortuary and funereal themes. Pastoral elegy emerged from a renewed interest in classical literature, and Bion's *Death of Adonis*, Virgil's *Eclogues* and Moschus' *Lament for Bion* (parts of which Wordsworth translated into English in 1788), provided elegiac templates for poets like Milton and Spenser, who found their references to shepherds and flocks assimilable with a Christian poetics. Mortuary elegy was more directly religious, but was marked by an obsessive fascination with graveyards, corpses, spectres, worms and owls. This kind of elegy was commonly used by graveyard poets such as Robert Blair, Edward Young and Thomas Gray, who each explored the tension between the horror of death and damnation and the consolation of divine redemption.

Related to the mortuary elegy was the funeral elegy, which served as both a public form (functioning as a visual broadside and displaying woodcuts of bones, skulls and hourglasses); and also as a private form (as a poem written by the individual mourner and thrown into the grave during the burial of the dead). One of the last known instances of this latter tradition occurred during the funeral of the Master of St John's, Cambridge in 1787, and was witnessed by Wordsworth who had just begun his degree there. Invited to write an elegy for the Master as a way of promoting his commitment to a poetic career, however, Wordsworth refused, claiming to have no personal intimacy with the deceased. He had written other elegiac poems, such as 'The Dog – An Idyllium' (1786), because he had felt genuinely close to the deceased animal; he was not prepared to undermine the form by addressing it to a man he did not know.

The domestic and shared experience of mourning, between a man and a dog, within communities, families and in the interaction between humans and nature, is central to Wordsworth's elegies, whether they are addressed to semi-fictionalized figures like 'Matthew' (which the poet sometimes spelled 'Mathew') and 'Lucy', or to real people, like his brother John and his daughter Catherine. In 'Elegy Written in the Same Place upon the Same Occasion' (1799), for example, Wordsworth mourns Matthew (assumed by critics to represent the Hawkshead headmaster, William Taylor), in a familiar and intimate manner, rejecting the artifice of elegiac convention. The narrator refuses to sob uncontrollably at Matthew's death, intimating instead: 'I feel more sorrow in a smile / Than in a waggon load of tears' (3–4). Similarly, Wordsworth domesticates the pastoral convention of introducing the grief of classical or biblical figures that mourn alongside the narrator. Where Milton summons Triton, Camus and St Peter to mourn his friend Edward King in *Lycidas* (1638), Wordsworth turns to ordinary villagers – 'ruddy damsels' (25), 'Mothers' (37), 'Staid men' (33), 'Old Women' (41) and 'sheep-curs' (49) – to elegize Matthew.

The communal and shared aspect of mourning characterizes many of Wordsworth's elegies, including those he wrote for John in 1805–6 ('To the Daisy (Sweet Flower!)', 'Distressful Gift! This Book Receives', 'When, to the Attractions of the Busy World', 'Elegiac Verses in Memory of My Brother, John Wordsworth' and 'Elegiac Stanzas Suggested by a Picture of Peele Castle'). In 'Elegiac Verses', for example, written just a few months after John's death, Wordsworth invokes 'me and mine' (19) as his fellow mourners, the communality of the family's grief enabling a collective consolation that protects him from the emotional paralysis of private mourning. In 'Elegiac Stanzas Suggested by a Picture of Peele Castle' (1806), however, written a year after John's death, Wordsworth is able to look back and note how, even though he was temporarily disabled by his grief, he has reflected enough on these feelings to turn them into joyful remembrance. John's death thus becomes a 'deep distress' that 'hath humanized my Soul' (36). Dorothy similarly reflected on and recollected her grief to come to terms with John's death:

> I see nothing that he would not have loved with me and enjoyed had
> he been by my side; and indeed, my consolations rather come to me in
> gusts of feeling, than are the quiet growth of my Mind. I know it will

not always be so – the time will come when the light of the setting Sun upon these mountain tops will be as heretofore a pure joy – not the same *gladness*, that can never be – but yet a joy even more tender. It will soothe me to know how happy *he* would have been could he have seen the same beautiful spectacle.[23]

The elegiac tone of Dorothy's letter, like that of Wordsworth's elegies, moves us because it invites us into an experience of already shared, and so transfigured grief that allows us to reflect on our own loss.

The elegy is an interpersonal and reciprocal form for Wordsworth, presenting strong emotions about the dead to elicit continued feeling in the living reader. He argued in *Essays upon Epitaphs* (1810) that the epitaph, a poem written for inscription on a grave, performed a similar function, preserving memories of the dead by providing a focal point for the living to mourn. 'Hence the parish-church in the stillness of the country', Wordsworth stated, 'is a visible centre of a community of the living and the dead', housing the tombstones on which epitaphs are inscribed and offering a physical space for the collective expression of grief (*PW*, II.56). It is the graveyard, and not the church that Wordsworth centralizes here, an open space in which 'the sorrowing hearts of the survivors' can find release by acknowledging that their specific thoughts about particular deceased individuals echo those of other mourners, and so are joined with them 'into one harmony by the general sympathy' (*PW*, II.53, 57).

Wordsworth liked epitaphs because they are concrete, material and written in a 'general language of humanity', always functioning as 'true' because they are 'hallowed by love – the joint offspring of the worth of the dead and the affections of the living!' (*PW*, II.57, 58). As Wordsworth argues, the graveyard visitor, seeing only inscriptions of 'faithful Wives, tender Husbands, dutiful Children, and good Men of all classes', might well ask, ' "Where are all the *bad* people buried?" ' (*PW*, II.63) or dismiss the epitaphs he or she reads as sentimental and poorly written. Yet for Wordsworth, the aesthetic of the epitaph should enable good feeling in the present, not to erase the faults or problems of the past, but so that the onlooker might feel 'tranquillised' and emotionally connect with fellow mourners. 'An epitaph is not a proud writing shut up for the studious', he claimed, but 'is exposed to all', the 'stooping old man', 'the child', 'the stranger', 'the friend': 'it is concerning all, and for all' (*PW*, II.59).

While Wordsworth wrote many epitaphs of his own, copied out assiduously by Dorothy to reinforce their communal aspect, his favourite epitaph consisted of only a name and two dates, its anonymity universalizing its appeal:

> In an obscure corner of a Country Church-yard I once [es]pied, half-overgrown with Hemlock and Nettles, a very small Stone laid upon

> the ground, bearing nothing more than the name of the Deceased
> with the date of birth and death, importing that it was an Infant which
> had been born one day and died the following. I know not how far
> the Reader may be in sympathy with me, but more awful thoughts of
> rights conferred, of hopes awakened, of remembrances stealing away or
> vanishing were imparted to my mind by that Inscription there before
> my eyes than by any other that it has ever been my lot to meet with
> upon a Tomb-Stone.   (*PW*, II.93)

The inscription, two dates, is a paradigmatic form of poetry for Wordsworth, its meanings sustained not by interpretive skill but through the non-linguistic context in which it is read. The particularly of *this* inscription on *this* grave in *this* churchyard in *this* community grants the numbers of these dates a meaning beyond intellectual inquiry, one that is instead sustained by the shared experiences and affections of those who stand before it. If we attempt to aestheticize or analyse these bereaved or sorrowful feelings without emotionally entering them, Wordsworth suggests, we abstract our words into that counterspirit with which we began the chapter, shutting individuals away inside a linguistic rather than lived world.

Silent poetry

For Wordsworth, then, successful poetry enables human feeling rather than cerebral critical commentary. In his own poetry he sought to shape readers through a gentle sensibility that made them into poets too, liberating them to fine-tune their feelings so that they could offer compassion to others. For him, the poet is:

> the rock of defence of human nature; an upholder and preserver,
> carrying every where with him relationship and love. In spite of
> difference of soil and climate, of language and manners, of laws and
> customs, in spite of things silently gone out of mind and things violently
> destroyed, the Poet binds together by passion and knowledge the vast
> empire of human society, as it is spread over the whole earth, and over all
> time. The objects of the Poet's thoughts are every where.   (*PW*, I.141)

The poet's objective is to humanize the world by drawing out its emotional aspect, reminding readers that what makes us unique is our shared capacity for feeling. John, for example, was a clumsy communicator, wrote no verse, and struggled to articulate his feelings in both public and private form. A letter to Mary, for example, in which he responds to her offer of a home where he would always be welcome after her marriage to his brother, is suggestive of John's capacity for a strong feeling he is impotent to express:

> I have been reading your Letter over & over again My dearest Mary till tears have come into my eyes & I known [sic] not how to express my[s] elf thou ar't [a] kind & dear creature. But wh<t>at ever fate Befal me I shall love to the last and bear thy<y> memory with me to the grave Thine affly John Wordsworth.[24]

This, his last surviving letter to his future sister-in-law, is indicative of those qualities in him Wordsworth most admired: patience, kindness, affection and, most of all, a love of poetry (the last two lines of John's letter include a reference to Wordsworth's poem 'Michael'). While John's attempts at communication are awkward, the depth of feeling expressed is genuine and full of meaning: there is nothing poetic in terms of sound or metre, but as an overflow of feeling the letter is model verse.

Wordsworth consequently called John a 'silent poet', inscribing the title on his grave at St Oswald's in Grasmere to encapsulate his admiration for John's sensitivity to nature and to those around him. For Wordsworth, the emotional activity that precedes composition of written poems is more valuable than the finished text (and we should remember that there are few poems in Wordsworth's collected works that he himself considered complete, consumed as he was in constant revisions of his poetry). Wordsworth's most affective poetic figures – the old man travelling, the old Cumberland beggar, Martha Ray, Goody Blake, Michael, the idiot boy, the leech gatherer, Emily Norton – are all silent poets who live between the felt experiences of life and their expression in words. These borderline people represent an insight and affective state that, because it cannot be verbalized, is disregarded by a 'talking world' that values intellectual, not emotional accomplishments (*P*, XII.172). The silent poet is coextensive with that valued most by Wordsworth, however, embodying, like John, compassion, receptivity and awareness. 'I can say nothing higher of my ever dear Brother', Wordsworth wrote to Beaumont, 'than that he was worthy of his Sister who is now weeping beside me, and of the friendship of Coleridge: meek, affectionate, silently enthusiastic, loving all quiet things, and a Poet in every thing but words.'[25]

In 'When First I Journeyed Hither' (1800), Wordsworth even addresses his brother John as:

> A silent Poet! from the solitude
> Of the vast Sea didst bring a watchful heart
> Still couchant, an inevitable ear
> And an eye practised like a blind man's touch.   (88–91)

If words are a counter-spirit to the expression of emotions, granting them a voice but then threatening to dissolve their experiential aspect by doing so, then the silent poet makes such feelings material, animated and incarnate without distorting them. He is like the gravestone on which the epitaph is inscribed, sustaining and manifesting emotion in a non-linguistic form. Wordsworth, by contrast, depended on language to evoke his experience of life's emotional content, but the poems that he wrote invariably 'derange', 'subvert', 'lay waste', 'vitiate' and 'dissolve' these experiences in curious and unfamiliar ways (*PW*, II.85). His constant revisions to these poems also exemplify his commitment to poetry as a fluid and changing form that confounds the reader intent on fixing the meaning of his work or discovering the 'standard' text. The next chapter explores Wordsworth's poetry by offering some suggestive readings to facilitate, rather than influence, your own interpretations of the varying and shifting meanings they comprise.

Works

Wordsworth's poems are strange. They address the relationship between nature and the self, but are not straightforwardly pastoral or biographical. They conjure shadowy and silent beings who appear from and disappear into rural landscapes, but reject the narrative demands of the Gothic or romance. They sometimes seem facile, leaving them vulnerable to satire and parody, but when looked at again betray an emotional complexity that lures us into political, ethical and moral questions. When Sara Hutchinson claimed to have disliked Wordsworth's poem 'The Leech-Gatherer' (1802) (later called 'Resolution and Independence'), Dorothy replied:

> When you happen to be displeased with what you suppose to be the tendency or moral of any poem which William writes, ask yourself whether you have hit upon the real tendency and true moral, and above all never think that he writes for no reason merely because a thing happened – and when you feel any poem of his to be tedious, ask yourself in what spirit it was written – whether merely to tell the tale and be through with it, or to illustrate a particular character or truth.[1]

John Keats similarly recognized the importance of going with the feeling evoked by Wordsworth's poetry rather than attempting to scrutinize or squeeze meaning out of it. He wrote that Wordsworth's skill resided in his capacity to lead us down 'dark passages. We see not the balance of good and evil; we are in a mist, we are now in that state, we feel the "Burden of the Mystery". 'Here', declares Keats, 'I must think Wordsworth is deeper than Milton ... He did not think into the human heart as Wordsworth has done.'[2] This focus on the heart offers readers a way into the profoundly sentient and discerning explorations of human experience within Wordsworth's poetry, steeped as they are in loss, alienation, isolation and fragmentation. From his classical school exercises, Gothic balladry and picturesque scene paintings, through to his political satires, lyrical ballads, epic narratives and final poems, Wordsworth sought to find a voice that might articulate his own story of loss and isolation and restore the self to wholeness through recourse to feeling.

'An Evening Walk' and 'Salisbury Plain'

In Wordsworth's early poems, however, access to such restorative feeling is precarious. The narrators of 'The Vale of Esthwaite' (1787), 'An Evening Walk' (1788–9) and 'Salisbury Plain' (1793), for example, attempt to confidently reflect on their moods, but instead appear detached from the world, desperately seeking answers to their feelings of alienation and loneliness. Wordsworth initially turned to the Gothic mode to frame this experience of uncertainty, a genre suited to exploring disturbed mental states, psychological extremes and death. 'The Vale of Esthwaite' combines Gothic with the sentimental to explore grief through a figure that wanders, entranced, through a valley. He is rapt by his own vivid impressions of what he sees – hypnotic waterfalls, smoke rising spirit-like and an imagined haunted castle through which he is led by a spectral 'grisly guide' (256). Here we witness the natural world embodying a spiritual energy that generates an inner experience in the narrator of self-consciousness and imaginative vision. This experience then makes possible a heightened relationship with specific moments – Wordsworth calls them 'spots' – that when recalled, invoke the emotions felt at those scenes.

In both 'The Vale' and 'An Evening Walk' we hear Wordsworth's deep sense that nature is not simply an external world designed by a creator God for human observation, but a dynamic power that vitalizes perception and provides a model for the development of the human mind. While the poems draw on pastoral and topographical poetic convention, they refuse to present the landscape as a map or scene and instead stress its variety. For that reason, nature becomes a gallery of fleeting objects and qualities that catch our eye: it is our emotional response to specificity that moves us through the scene, not the landscape itself. Wordsworth's 'Descriptive Sketches' (1793), which trace a walk through the French and Swiss Alps, also underline this changeable and transitory element of nature by switching, sketch-like, between places, seasons, sublime scenes, picturesque vistas and different times of day.

'An Evening Walk', however, focuses our attention on the evening, a shadowy interval between day and night in which we are forced to adjust our perception of the world and so feel and imagine what we see more intensely. While the poem is loco-descriptive (a genre that pays careful attention to a specific place or locality), it internalizes this idiom, transforming it into a mental action that moves us through the poem emotionally and spatially. Wordsworth thus goes against a late eighteenth-century trend to categorize and label nature, popularized by natural historians such as Gilbert White, by refusing to dissect the landscape and invoking instead the mystery of what he sees: the 'liquid gold' brooks (172), 'half seen form of Twilight' (334), 'Fair Spirits' (347), 'cottage smoke' (369) and watery music of the 'glimmering deeps' (349).[3] He also domesticates this pastoral scene by developing the affectionate relationships he sees around him in the natural world, between dogs, horses, ducks, pikes and herons. Wordsworth even praises a 'Fair swan!' (241), not because of her conventional beauty, but because she appears to him to be an exemplary mother to her cygnets.

Yet Wordsworth's presentation of an idyllic natural world in 'An Evening Walk' does not simply summon a feeling of stability. It rather directs our attention to his experience of time passing, the poet declaring from line 1 that he is 'Far from my dearest Friend' (Dorothy) in a landscape haunted by shadows indicative of his isolation. Human presences seem displaced in this world of profound stillness, the female vagrant, in contrast with the restful mother swan, desperate, frozen and unable to 'thaw' the little fingers of her children (281). Yet it is with the beggar that Wordsworth's narrator connects himself, both through a compassionate language of sensibility, and also through a shared attachment to an unfamiliar landscape. Whether we read her, with the feminist critic Mary Jacobus, as a sentimentalized trope, or with the new historicist Alan Liu as a symbol of history, the beggar unsettles the poem's aesthetic calm by representing a homeless population that must remain outdoors even after the poem's shift into night-time. Wordsworth remained preoccupied with the female vagrant in several other poems too: 'Salisbury Plain' (1793); 'Adventures on Salisbury Plain' (1795); 'The Female Vagrant' (*Lyrical Ballads*, 1798); and 'Guilt and Sorrow; or, Incidents upon Salisbury Plain' (1842).[4]

The Salisbury Plain poems explore the relationship between two itinerant figures as they wander over the desolate, chalky landscape. They are engaged in both a spiritual quest, symbolized by Salisbury's famous landmark, Stonehenge; and also a social one, signified by the plain's notoriety as a once thriving agricultural centre now destroyed by industrialization. The reader is also alerted to the poem's political content by its Spenserian romance form (eight lines of iambic pentameter plus an Alexandrine line), one traditionally associated with protest narratives. The narrator's cry in 'Salisbury Plain' (1793) – 'Oh! what can war but endless war still breed?' (509) – confirms this, drawing our attention to a landscape ravaged by the effects of capitalism and war. In this, the earliest draft of the poem, we encounter a traveller caught in a storm 'beneath night's starless gloom' (110) and whose 'only bed' is 'the wet cold ground' (63). Desperate to escape his 'night-terrors' (124), he is mysteriously called across the plain to a 'lonely Spital' (123) lit up by the moon's 'wan dead light' (140), which casts a ghostly glow on its female inhabitant. Both traveller and vagrant seem almost zombie-like in appearance, frightened spectres paralysed by their dread of the dark and Gothic plain.

Yet the scene that develops between them is intimate and gentle. The traveller helps the vagrant to loosen the dressings on her 'wounds' (203), and she relates to him the details of her fall into poverty following the deaths of her husband and children in the American war. The unbinding of bandages and stories connects them in a shared experience of mourning, and they humanize each other through a reciprocal compassion, talking through the stormy night so that the new day seems 'fresh' (333) and 'Tempered' by 'sweet words of hope' (342). In the morning, the two figures appear as comrades, setting out across the plain together. Their mutual trust is rewarded by the appearance of a 'smoking cottage' (410), a potential shelter and symbol of the home the two already have in each other's company. Wordsworth does not imply that this sympathetic identification restores their loss, however. He closes the poem with a plea to those in power to end 'Exile, Terror, Bonds, and Force' (515) by reforming the Poor Law, recalling William Godwin's practical political philosophy of social justice.

By the time Wordsworth came to revise the poem as 'Adventures on Salisbury Plain' (1795), however, he had lost faith in the Godwinian project. The government had not only ignored the requests of reformers, but had aggravated the situation by passing treason laws (the Treasonable Practices Bill and Seditious Meetings Bill) granting them the power to control and survey, but not help, the homeless. Godwin's rationalism seemed ill equipped to deal with the psychological damage injustice stirred up in individuals, and the revised 'Salisbury Plain' presents a darker and more conflicted traveller unable to find solace in companionship. Now a vagrant sailor discharged from service without pay, the traveller murders an innocent man for money (97) before meeting the female vagrant with whom he is now unable to create any sympathetic bond, obsessed as he is by guilt and anger. 'His thoughts, still cleaving to the murder'd man' (597) anaesthetize all feeling in him, and it is only when he encounters an argument between a husband and wife that the sailor is able to invoke the 'bond of nature' (661) as a basis on which the conflicted family might reconcile.

Wordsworth opposes these individual acts of forgiveness and empathy to the abstract and cruel judgements of society and the state, the sailor's wife, whom we meet at the end of the poem, shunned from her community as a consequence of the murder and now homeless, sick and impoverished. While she exonerates her husband and dies peacefully with 'A sudden joy surprized expiring thought' (777), he is hanged in chains for his crime. We know from the *Sonnets upon the Punishment of Death* (1841) that Wordsworth was not categorically opposed to the death penalty, but he is concerned here to highlight the tension between the sailor's mistreatment by a nation he fought to defend and the apparently rational justice of his final sentence. The same critique of Godwin's inflexible rationalism is repeated in Wordsworth's five-act tragedy, *The Borderers* (1796–7). Yet it is in 'The Ruined Cottage' (1797) that Wordsworth seems to find an answer to Godwin in nature, a location in which the fractured individual might finally be repaired.

'The Ruined Cottage' and 'The Discharged Soldier'

'The Ruined Cottage' (1797–8) is the first poem in which Wordsworth explicitly connects nature to the human imagination, the hero a Bible-reading pantheist rather than a rational Godwinian. 'Pantheism' was the belief that God was immanent in every aspect of the material universe ('pan' – all; 'theos' – God), a 'sense sublime', Wordsworth suggested, that was 'deeply interfused' in 'all things' ('Tintern Abbey', 95–102). The interconnectedness of 'all things' is central to 'The Ruined Cottage', a poem that embodies a vision of equilibrium forwarded by the pantheist character – the Pedlar – also known as 'the wanderer' or 'Armytage' in revised versions. The poem relates a conversation between a poet figure, who represents Wordsworth and his readers, and the Pedlar. As the two men sit in the doorway of a now ruined and overgrown cottage, the Pedlar begins to relate the tragic tale of a prior tenant, a war-widow called Margaret.

Margaret's story begins after a poor harvest exacerbated by the impact of war on the rural economy. In an attempt to provide for his family, Margaret's husband Robert joins the army, leaving his enlistment pay for them on the windowsill. As time elapses, however, Margaret begins to fear that Robert will never return, and anxiously seeks news of her absent husband from passers-by. One of these passers-by is the Pedlar, who, during regular visits to Margaret, witnesses her progressive decline into depression as she obsessively waits for

Robert inside the crumbling cottage. Her mental health deteriorates further when her eldest child leaves the household to become a 'serving-boy' (346) for the parish and her baby dies, leaving her isolated in 'unquiet widowhood' (447) and paralysed by grief. Fixated on Robert's return, Margaret locks herself into a period of painful anticipation:

> And so she lived
> Through the long winter, reckless and alone,
> Till this reft house by frost, and thaw, and rain
> Was sapped; and when she slept the nightly damps
> Did chill her breast, and in the stormy day
> Her tattered clothes were ruffled by the wind
> Even at the side of her own fire. Yet still
> She loved this wretched spot, nor would for worlds
> Have parted hence.   (480–8)

The Pedlar attempts to alleviate the bleakness of his story in a conciliatory postscript added to the poem in 1799. Here he teaches the poet figure how to manage his desolate reaction to Margaret's tale by developing sympathy with the natural world. Leaning on the garden-gate to the cottage, the narrator remains overcome by the tragedy, but notices that he is lifted from the paralysis Margaret suffered by reflecting on the verdant beauty of her home now covered with 'silent overgrowings' (506). The Pedlar urges him to notice that ' "what we feel of sorrow and despair / From ruin and from change" ' (520–1) dissipates when we focus our attention on those feelings as a way of bringing us into the present moment. By noticing that grief becomes ' "an idle dream that could not live / Where meditation was" ' (523–4), the Pedlar releases himself and the poet into a warmed-up world made comfortable by the 'mellow radiance' (527) of the sun and steadied by silence. Their serenity comes from a complete acceptance of the moment in which they reside, following nature's example as it embraces the damaged cottage with 'goose-berry trees' (57) and 'willow boughs' (61), but refrains from attempting to fix or change the situation in which it crumbles away.

Some readers find the addendum to the poem objectionable. Thomas De Quincey, for example, berated Wordsworth for refusing to deal 'with intense realities': the Pedlar does not offer Margaret material help, fails to report her troubles to the Parish, and never writes to the War Office for news of Robert.[5] Yet Wordsworth suggests that Margaret's grief is a state of mind that is restored not by money or parliamentary intervention, but through attention to the relationship between emotional and material life. Margaret is trapped in her grief because she refuses or is unable to work through her feelings or learn that the patient form of joy nature intimates is constantly available. She no longer cares for herself or others, and is thus imprisoned within her own emotional drama.

Wordsworth emphasizes how easy it is to surrender to grief by suggesting that the poet almost falls into a similar psychological state to Margaret, initially responding to her story with a 'heartfelt chillness' (213) that freezes his emotions and threatens to block sympathy. He is an emotional mirror of Margaret at the beginning of the story, unwilling to reflect on his surroundings, blind to nature's influence and so only able to encounter the landscape as bare and hostile, beset as he is by flying insects and 'seeds of bursting gorse' (26). The Pedlar, on the other hand, reconciled to his environment, claims that he can ' "see around me here / Things which you cannot see" ' (68–7), and proves his love for Margaret by offering emotional, not fiscal, support. His at-one-ness with the tranquillity of nature allows him to understand Margaret's death as part of a bigger picture. It is this faithful belief in the power of fortune and repose that ultimately heals his sorrow.

We might also argue that in refraining to label Margaret as 'other' ('poor', 'widow', 'disturbed' and so on), the Pedlar sets up the idea of a shared human body in which everyone deserves compassion. By privileging communal feeling, the poem suggests that the mistreatment of any individual damages the whole of society, thus producing a staunchly anti-war message. This message is echoed in a poem called 'The Discharged Soldier' (1798), a fragment poem later incorporated into *The Prelude* (*P*, IV.364–504). While Margaret cannot translate her despondency into joy through community or nature, the Robert-like figure of 'The Discharged Soldier' does move out of his isolation, accepting the humanizing actions of the narrator as evidence of his personal self-worth.

The narrator of the poem meets the discharged soldier at night while walking through the Lakes. Noticing a mysterious figure 'clad in military garb' (54) and propped up on a milestone, the narrator for a moment thinks he has seen a ghost 'ghastly in the moonlight' (51). Unnerved by the apparition, the narrator initially reads the soldier as inhuman and disconnected from life ('He was alone, / Had no attendant, neither dog, nor staff', 61–2), and hears him 'murmuring sounds as if in pain / Or of uneasy thought (70–1). Yet when he approaches the soldier and talks with him his perspective changes: he notices both that the soldier does carry 'a oaken staff' (116) after all, and also that his voice sounds, not grieved, but 'at ease and much relieved' (130). In turn, the soldier is humanized by this attention, at first tentatively engaging with the narrator, who offers him lodgings with a local labourer, and then softening as he is welcomed inside the cottage whereupon he is finally able 'To speak with a reviving interest / Till then unfelt' (169–70).

The soldier embodies a kind of affective strength in the poem, refusing to succumb to self-interest (he feels no sense of entitlement despite his efforts abroad) and moving out of despondency by acknowledging the narrator's expression of sympathy. Emotionally touched by the encounter, the narrator remains momentarily arrested outside the cottage door the soldier has disappeared behind, feeling his heart settle before they part. Like the milestone the soldier is propped upon, the cottage door offers the narrator a material object on which to project his feelings, leaving him free to reflect on them. It is as if Wordsworth's 'borderers', those marginal, dispossessed individuals who also populate the *Lyrical Ballads*, possess an insightful ability to emotionally respond to the world that teach Wordsworth's poet-narrators how to feel even when 'life's business' is not a 'summer mood' ('Resolution and Independence', 37). The idea of a sympathetic universe may no longer have been tenable in the turmoil of the 1790s, but the power of the sympathetic imagination to transform alienation into affection was possible, as Wordsworth explored in his first major collection of poems.

The *Lyrical Ballads*

The *Lyrical Ballads* (1798) continue to examine the capacity of the poetic imagination to repair the effects of human suffering and mortality. Wordsworth achieved this by creating a new kind of writing that fused the musicality and emotion of the lyric with the story-telling capacity of the ballad. He planned to write these poems collaboratively with Coleridge, and while the two poets achieved only some minor teamwork on 'The Rime of the Ancyent Marinere' (1798) and 'We Are Seven' (1798), the collection nevertheless arose from the communal experiences the two men shared with Dorothy in Alfoxden. It was Wordsworth, however, who used the volume to explore the idea that suffering provokes a condition of temporary alienation in us, from which we move out, not by stagnating in such misery, but by using our sadness to motivate us to be watchful of the suffering of others. Each poem confirms that suffering is a fact of the human condition, but suggests that we cope with this by attending to the particularities of people in difficult situations by offering them support, empathy and sympathy.

If alienation and affection are the key forms of opposed experience in the *Lyrical Ballads*, then they reveal that while suffering is a constant in human life it always has the potential to engender sympathy. This is what Wordsworth means when he suggests we can translate grief into joy through meditation (that is, attention to feeling). Hence the first poem of the 1798 edition, Coleridge's 'Ancyent Marinere', unsettles and disorients us, a position from which we then read a series of tales focused on human injustice and sorrow before arriving at the volume's final and distinctly consoling 'Tintern Abbey'. As 'experiments', these poems invite us to find our own meanings, but their simple and stripped-down forms also guide us into a state of basic and habitual feeling that fine-tunes our emotional and interpretive responses to the chronology of the contents.

In the 1800 two-volume edition, for example, Wordsworth placed together the gentle and percipient old man travelling, forsaken Indian woman and shepherd of 'The Last of the Flock' (1798) against the disenchanted and impatient William Brathwaite in 'Lines Left upon a Seat in a Yew-tree' (1797), an example of someone who refuses to reconnect himself to the world through feeling. This sequence is then followed by a number of narrative poems ('Goody Blake and Harry Gill', 'The Thorn', 'We Are Seven', 'Anecdote for Fathers', 'The Female Vagrant'), that give the reader space to think further about the character types Wordsworth both values and denigrates. The reader finally encounters a series of meditative fragments ('There Was a Boy', 'A Slumber Did My Spirit Seal', also written in 1798) and blank verses ('The Brothers', 'The Old Cumberland Beggar', 'Michael') that stimulate contemplation.

Wordsworth thus shapes a reading experience designed to strengthen our affections for each other and so bond society together through feeling. As war, social upheaval, injustice and the effects of capitalism and industrialization break these bonds, however, we are plunged into a state of alienation, in which our experience of life feels fragmentary, transient, lonely and 'unnatural'. Wordsworth suggests that nature grants humans a stable ground on which to redress this alienation by engaging in shared, repeated and 'natural' experience that produces affection. For those unable to access nature, severed from its effects either by geography or emotional numbness, poetry provides an alternative ground for the expression and recollection of emotional experience. The *Lyrical Ballads* are intended both to repair the nation's social fabric by addressing its emotional health, and also to dissipate tension between individuals (not least the joint authors, whose emotional if not material collaboration had highlighted their differences as well as kinship).

Perhaps this is why Wordsworth felt so uncomfortable about the inclusion of Coleridge's 'Ancyent Marinere' and 'Christabel', poems that record a movement from incident to a heightened sensation that short-circuits the process of reflection necessary to the experience of meditative feeling. Wordsworth too shows us figures caught in moments of intense, almost unbearable, feeling, but in contrast to Coleridge, he traces the source of such emotion to everyday occurrences and objects. While Coleridge thinks about ghost ships and lesbian vampires, Wordsworth is concerned with lost sheep and old trees. For him, there is something fundamental and compelling about the extraordinary feelings ordinary people have about workaday matters. Wordsworth enables his readers to engage with and so respect these extraordinary feelings by sustaining and dignifying the experience of them in the poems that comprise the volume.

'The Last of the Flock', for example, presents us with an image of a 'sturdy' but 'sad' (9) shepherd, weeping in a public road with the body of a dead lamb in his arms. We feel his desperate love for the flock, not only because of the implied economic ruin such loss brings, but because we witness the gradual build of his trauma as his sheep die, one by one:

> 'They dwindled, Sir, sad sight to see!
> From ten to five, from five to three,
> A lamb, a wether, and a ewe;
> And then at last, from three to two;
> And of my fifty, yesterday
> I had but only one,
> And here it lies upon my arm,
> Alas! and I have none;
> To-day I fetched it from the rock;
> It is the last of all my flock'.   (91–100)

The stark simplicity of these lines together with the shepherd's raw feeling might evoke more than clear-cut compassion in readers, however. Rather than being moved or touched by this portrait, Wordsworth recognized, readers might instead encounter 'feelings of strangeness and awkwardness' (*PW*, I.123), finding the scene oddly comic or simply wanting to run away and hide from this crying man (as the narrator of *The Prelude* does when he first meets the discharged soldier). He thus deliberately refuses to prompt or control reader response to his anonymous and publicly distraught wanderers throughout the *Lyrical Ballads*: should readers feel pity and fraternal feeling for the weeping shepherd and his fellow mourners or embarrassment and revulsion?

Wordsworth's ballads of lament (sometimes called 'complaints') are so unmediated that readers might even waiver between these two extremes before coming to the necessary recognition that they are connected emotional states, one leading to the other. Without this realization, readers risk assuming a subject position similar to the cartoonish narrators of 'We Are Seven' or 'The Idiot Boy', who condescend to rather than contemplate the people they describe. Wishing to keep his readers 'in the company of flesh and blood' (*PW*, I.131), Wordsworth shows us the material effects of both compassion (which heals damaged communities) and failed sympathy (which exacerbates social fragmentation). Neither is presented didactically but the moral implications of withholding sympathy are driven home in poems like 'The Convict', 'The Female Vagrant', 'The Thorn' and 'Goody Blake and Harry Gill'.

Wordsworth called 'Goody Blake and Harry Gill' the 'rudest' poem (*PW*, I.150) in the collection, combining the ballad and dramatic monologue form to energize its strange narrative and the uncertainty of its details, coming as they do from a verbose, near hysterical narrator. The first poem written explicitly for the *Lyrical Ballads*, it tells a story about a wealthy landowner called Harry Gill, who persecutes an old, impoverished weaver called Goody Blake. As she works through each day and night, Goody can barely afford the candles that light her shelter, and, chilled to her shaking bones by an especially harsh winter, she is forced to glean a few sticks for her fire from one of Harry's hedges. The act, while necessary, is illegal, and Harry lays siege to her one night 'behind a rick of barley' (73), springing out at her 'with a shout' (87): 'And fiercely by the arm he took her, / And by the arm he held her fast, / And fiercely by the arm he shook her, / And cried, "I've caught you then at last!"' (89–92). The violence of his arrest disrupts the ballad and the reader is suddenly plunged into a dreadful silence, the metre tip-toeing around Harry's reaction to Goody's prayer:

> She prayed, her withered hand uprearing,
> While Harry held her by the arm –
> 'God! who art never out of hearing,
> Oh may he never more be warm!'
> The cold, cold moon above her head,
> Thus on her knees did Goody pray,
> Young Harry heard what she had said,
> And icy cold he turned away.   (97–104)

The spectacle of the emaciated Goody invoking God with her shrivelled hand is disturbing because of its immediate impact on Harry: the episode is dependent on the 'power of the human imagination' (*PW*, I.150), but it is difficult not to believe that Harry has been cursed.

As he layers on coat after coat in an attempt to get warm, Harry is transformed into an impotent and skeletal old man, rattling away like the poem's metre:

> 'Twas all vain, a useless matter,
> And blankets were about him pinned;
> Yet still his jaws and teeth they clatter,
> Like a loose casement in the wind.
> And Harry's flesh it fell away;
> And all who see him say, 'tis plain,
> That, live as long as live he may,
> He never will be warm again.   (113–120)

Harry is now muted by the consequences of his miserly behaviour, shaking too much to move or speak: 'evermore his teeth they chatter, / Chatter, chatter, chatter still' (3–4). By contrast, Goody is vocally powerful: her curse works because she has genuinely suffered, her authentic feelings a source for her imaginative power. In Adela Pinch's reading of the poem, Harry even disintegrates into a parody of Goody: he is 'pinned' to his bed like an old woman and his shattered body is frozen under a mountain of blankets. Unlike Goody, however, he lacks the imaginative ability to think himself out of his situation, an 'automatic, seemingly agentless generator of metrical sound'.[6] Goody may well be frail and weak, trapped as she is in a state of extreme penury, but she is linguistically strong, controlling what she says by occasionally falling silent and suggesting, like Wordsworth's verses on John, that it is more important to feel one's circumstances than to translate them into words.

The disconcertingly silent Martha Ray in 'The Thorn' has little of the vocal power of Goody Blake, but she does share with her an emotional connection to a natural world that punishes those who judge, alienate or harm the weak. Like Harry Gill, those who do victimize or unjustly reproach others tend to struggle with expression in Wordsworth's ballads: the retired sea captain who narrates 'The Thorn' flounders in his attempts to articulate anything of substance (repeating phrases such as 'I cannot tell', 'I never heard', 'They say', 'More know I not', 'I cannot think', 'I did not speak', 'some will say', 'I do not think' and so on); while the local community that shuns Martha becomes obsessed with details to which it has no access. As a result, all the reader gathers from the story is that around twenty years before the poem's narration, Martha Ray fell in love with Stephen Hill, became engaged to him and then fell pregnant while he unthinkingly married another suitor. Her child, however, is never seen, an absence that incites the cruel gossip of a community that, rather than counsel or assist Martha, viciously accuse her of killing her baby (by hanging, drowning or stabbing, they conjecture) and so drive her out of the village into the mountains, where she resides forever crying " 'Oh misery! oh misery! / Oh woe is me! oh misery!' " (65–6).

Yet the poem's focus is on a little spot in the landscape comprised of an old, grey and knotted thorn, a 'little muddy pond' (30) and a 'beauteous' half-foot high 'hill of moss' (36) – the setting for Martha's grief and a scene into which she is organically integrated. Her 'scarlet cloak' (179) near conceals her against the blood-red moss (221) of the mound, and an observer might even mistake her for the thorn itself, it is implied, semi-human and 'Not higher than a two-years' child' (5). The captain nonetheless sets out to determine the 'real' details of her predicament, dissatisfied and appalled by the village's lurid reading of Martha as a killer and the pretty mound as an 'infant's grave' (52). He describes what he can see of the scene in the mountains in meticulous detail (bringing along his nautical telescope through which to view it), claims to have measured the muddy pond ("Tis three feet long, and two feet wide', 33), and becomes mesmerized by the 'mossy network' of 'lovely colours' 'woven' by nature into the mound, 'olive-green and scarlet bright', 'Green, red, and pearly white' (38–48).

Yet unlike the Pedlar's benevolent relationship to Margaret in 'The Ruined Cottage', the captain's interest in Martha is voyeuristic and unthoughtful. As Wordsworth writes in his supplementary 'Note' to 'The Thorn', the retired sailor can imagine her plight, but lacks the emotional awareness that would 'excite' his imagination into compassion. Frustrated in his attempts to fix the details of the story, he surrenders to superstition, confiding to the reader that 'Some say, if to the pond you go' (225), 'A baby and a baby's face' (228) will peer up from beneath the murky water. The 'Some say' of this disclosure, however, informs the reader that he personally is prohibited from this supernatural vision by nature itself, a force that also prohibits the villagers' gruesome desire to dig up the bones of Martha's dead baby:

> And some had sworn an oath that she
> Should be to public justice brought;
> And for the little infant's bones
> With spades they would have sought.
> But then the beauteous hill of moss
> Before their eyes began to stir;
> And for full fifty yards around,
> The grass it shook upon the ground.   (232–9)

Nature protects Martha here, shaking the ground when the villagers try and dig up her baby's grave. It ceremoniously covers the grave with decorative mosses, muddies the water in which snooping telltales hunt for a glimpse of her dead child, and derails the captain's trip to the mountains by conjuring 'mist and rain, and storm and rain', 'And then the wind!' (188, 190). While the captain separates himself from the mob-like vengeance the community enacts, he remains impotent to assist Martha because, like the villagers, his disconnection from the natural world immobilizes his sympathetic faculty.

The captain's inability to engage in the reflection required to sympathize with Martha is also apparent in the poem's rapid pace, the speed of the metre granting it a manic feel that blocks meditation. By contrast, the slow and subdued poem, 'Old Man Travelling', creates exactly the right conditions in which to think and feel. Unlike the captain, the old man travelling is entirely at one with nature, the 'little hedge-row birds, / That peck along the road' (1–2) undisturbed by the mild and patient pace of his journey to visit his son in hospital. His emotional being is so calm and profound that he 'moves / With thought', 'insensibly subdued / To settled quiet' (6–8). His love for his son is instinctive like nature's response to Martha's suffering. Wordsworth uses this poem to suggest that only those closest to nature can begin to repeat its kindness. The child in 'We Are Seven', Betty Foy in 'The Idiot Boy' and the shepherd in 'The Last of the Flock' are also close to nature and so able to intuitively feel for those close to them.

Yet Wordsworth was keenly aware that many middle-class readers of the *Lyrical Ballads* might find these poems simple and crude precisely because they suffer from the kind of emotional illiteracy within which his most detached and unthinking narrators – of 'The Thorn', 'Simon Lee, the old Huntsman', 'The Mad Mother' – are stuck. This unconscious state, born of a refusal to reflect on life, is one from which Wordsworth himself awoke during his traumatic experiences in France. The final poem in the volume consequently works to record his awakening to the importance of reflection as it embodies the feeling he hopes readers will develop by using his poems as a training ground for meditative and emotional practice.

'Lines Written a Few Miles above Tintern Abbey, on Revisiting the Banks of the Wye during a Tour, July 13, 1798' is consciously dated on the eve of Bastille Day, which marks the beginning of the French Revolution. Placed at the end of the *Lyrical Ballads*, the poem answers the other poems, suggesting that the social hardships presented so far might be solved, not by a violent revolution such as that which failed in France, but by a revolution in feeling. The lyrical tone of the poem commences this revolution, one used to convey the poet's devotion not only to nature but also to Dorothy, who is invoked as a model of perception, feeling, thought and reflection. She is as much the recipient of Wordsworth's prayer – 'Nature never did betray / The heart that loved her' (123–4) – as the natural landscape, teaching her brother how to feel both by becoming aware of the 'mind that is within us' (127) and also by opening him to the 'chearful faith' (134) of quiet being.

This process is not immediate, of course, which is why Wordsworth looks back on the 'five summers, with the length / Of five long winters!' (1–2) that have passed since his last visit to the Wye Valley with Robert Jones. During this interim, Wordsworth intimates, he learned to make sense of daily life by paying attention to the experiences it comprises, acknowledging and then thinking about his emotional response to these experiences by reflecting on them. By summoning memories of nature, specifically the sycamores, hedgerows, 'woods and copses' (13) that frame the ruined abbey, Wordsworth creates a lens through which he can see his world as a series of 'forms of beauty' (24), producing in him 'sensations sweet, / Felt in the blood, and felt along the heart, / And passing even into my purer mind, / With tranquil restoration' (28–31).

This meditative technique does not idealize the world he encounters, as the sharp social content of the ballads attest. It does, however, allow him to remain steady in each moment, painful and joyful alike, and see 'with an eye made quiet by the power / Of harmony' (48–9). This sense of imaginative vision enables Wordsworth to 'see into the life of things' (50), developing a perspective or way of looking that registers the experiential and emotional content of the world over and above its visual aspects:

> For I have learned
> To look on nature, not as in the hour
> Of thoughtless youth, but hearing oftentimes
> The still, sad music of humanity,
> Nor harsh nor grating, though of ample power
> To chasten and subdue. And I have felt
> A presence that disturbs me with the joy
> Of elevated thoughts; a sense sublime
> Of something far more deeply interfused,
> Whose dwelling is the light of setting suns,
> And the round ocean, and the living air,
> And the blue sky, and in the mind of man,
> A motion and a spirit, that impels
> All thinking things, all objects of all thought,
> And rolls through all things.   (89–103)

Focused on the feeling nature triggers in him, Wordsworth has to remind his reader that he is 'still / A lover of the meadows and the woods' (103–4) and a 'worshipper of Nature' (153), committed to its material environment as a foundation for human relationships. The shared respect he and Dorothy have for the landscape enhances its value for Wordsworth, allowing him to experience the 'warmer love' (155) of his sister, and also the 'holier love' (156) of the shepherd-like divinity that he feels is immanent in nature, one that 'restoreth' the 'soul' by making us 'lie down in green pastures' (Psalm 23.2–3).

For some critics, however, the restorative message of 'Tintern Abbey' is problematic, nature subsumed by the power of the imagination, sensory vision lost but not properly mourned and the poem's endless exclamation marks creating a forced tone that betrays Wordsworth's doubts concerning the very process of restoration he outlines. Intent on preserving nature as the grounds for human renewal, however, Wordsworth continued to explore the relationship between them in the expanded two-volume *Lyrical Ballads* (1800). The next sections read works included in this revised volume, specifically the haunting poems on intermediate beings that seem so much part of nature that they dissolve into it; and the powerful blank-verse narratives, 'Michael' and 'The Brothers', where the land assumes a character of its own.

Lucy and 'The Danish Boy'

'Lucy' is one of Wordsworth's most unnerving poetic figures. The poems in which she mysteriously lingers are toneless and hypnotic, and the narrator refuses to declare either what kind of experience Lucy evokes for him or how we as readers as supposed to respond. Wordsworth never formally grouped his 'Lucy' poems, but critics suggest that several of his verses share a recurrent fascination with a spirit-like girl. These poems include: the 1798 'Strange Fits of Passion Have I Known', 'She Dwelt among th' Untrodden Ways' and 'A Slumber Did My Spirit Seal'; 'Three Years She Grew in Sun and Shower' (written in 1799 and included in the 1800 *Lyrical Ballads*); and 'I Travelled among Unknown Men' (written in 1801 and published in the 1815 *Poems*). The genesis of all of these poems can be traced back to Wordsworth's winter trip to Goslar with Dorothy, a grim and isolating experience reflected in the otherworldly feel of the poems. Coleridge even suggests that the 'Lucy' group emerge from 'some gloomier moment' in which Wordsworth had 'fancied the moment in which his sister might die'. Wordsworth, however, claimed that he wrote them in 'self-defence' against his feelings of alienation in Germany, and their love-poem– epitaph form grants them an unearthliness that leaves the reader as dislocated and shaken as the narrator.[7]

This unsettled tone is compounded by the absence of the name 'Lucy' from the poems: as the narrator of 'She Dwelt among th' Untrodden Ways' states, the girl is more a 'Violet' (5) or a 'star' (7) than a human being. Moreover, the language used to address her is impeded and ambiguous, defamiliarizing us from our reading experience. We are pushed to see and hear the poems in a non-linear and non-rational way, like Lucy herself, who is rolled out of her own consciousness and into nature:

> A slumber did my spirit seal;
> I had no human fears:
> She seemed a thing that could not feel
> The touch of earthly years.
>
> No motion has she now, no force;
> She neither hears nor sees,
> Roll'd round in earth's diurnal course
> With rocks and stones and trees.

Nature takes over the role of mourning from the narrator here, integrating Lucy into its continuum just as the moon in 'Strange Fits of Passion' appears to crush Lucy as it drops from the night sky onto earth (24). In both these poems the narrator seems more concerned with the fact he *is* grieving than *why* he is grieving. The frantic ' "O mercy!" to myself I cried, / "If Lucy should be dead!" ' (27–8) of 'Strange Fits of Passion' echoes through the narrator's panic in 'A Slumber Did My Spirit Seal', triggered by an anxiety that his human capacity for fear has been stolen and replaced by something more terrifying. He is psychologically paralysed by Lucy's apparent death, the girl at once motionless and frozen even as she undulates in the iambic sound of 'rocks and stones and trees' (8). His experience of loving and losing Lucy is at once public (we are vividly aware of the intensity of grief expressed in the poems) and extraordinarily private (the details are so obscured that we are almost forced to invent the details of Lucy's narrative and in doing so perhaps reflect back on our own capacity for mourning).

That some Victorian readers naively believed Lucy was a real girl whom Wordsworth had murdered in a 'fit of passion' attests to the lengths to which readers are prepared to go to avoid contemplating or experiencing feelings of loss.[8] Modern commentators similarly sidestep the poems' emotional extremity by suggesting that while Wordsworth might not be a murderer, he did symbolically desire to kill his guilt over abandoning Annette in France or his incestuous love for his sister. We might consider instead that the poems portray, in arresting slow motion, the operation of the mind when exercised by pure fear, or, as Wordsworth wrote in the 'Preface', 'the manner in which we associate ideas in a state of excitement' (*PW*, I.123–4). It is as if Wordsworth wishes to stimulate different emotional states in the reader, such as panic, terror, sorrow and love, and allow us to really experience these states, albeit safely within the limits of the ballad form. Lucy becomes pure emotion in order that we might learn how to feel.

Wordsworth continued to experiment with the representation of pure emotion in 'The Danish Boy' (1799), its protagonist described as a 'thing', a 'shadow' and a 'spirit'. He is secluded, almost entombed, within the confines of an 'open dell' (5), hidden from human view 'Between two sister moorland rills' (1). While we might comfortably sympathize with Goody Blake or Martha Ray, the vague and imprecise Danish boy ruffles rather than moves us. He is 'a form of flesh and blood' (24), but also a ghost who haunts the dell he inhabits. Wordsworth later added a note to the poem explaining that the boy was a prince, who, taking refuge from battle in a stone hut, was murdered by the inhabitants for his belongings. As a victim of human brutality, nature protects the boy as he haunts the dell, avenging him by destroying other objects around him: the tree is 'tempest-stricken' (6) and the hut cracked apart by lightning, but he remains untouched, 'A thing no storm can e'er destroy, / The shadow of a Danish Boy' (10–11).

Like Martha Ray, who is almost indistinguishable from the thorn, the Danish boy grows into nature, his princely clothing made of raven-black fur, his helmet 'vernal' (32), his face blooming as if covered with flowers while his voice 'warbles' (52) like a bird. He is the 'darling and the joy' (38) not of any human community, but of the 'flocks upon the neighbouring hill' (39) where 'mountain-ponies' 'prick their ears' (41) to hear him sing and play the harp:

> The lovely Danish Boy is blest
> And happy in his flowery cove:
> From bloody deeds his thoughts are far;
> And yet he warbles songs of love,
> That seem like songs of war,
> For calm and gentle is his mien;
> Like a dead Boy he is serene.   (49–55)

This final verse intensifies the poem's eeriness by betraying both the narrator's physical proximity to the boy (he can hear him singing), but also his emotional detachment from him (he cannot determine whether the songs he hears address love or war). Only by emotionally entering the state of serenity the boy occupies might the narrator have a chance of accessing the lyric tone of these songs, just as we as readers must hear Wordsworth's own songs in a state of quietude to access their emotional content.

Wordsworth suggested that his readers might best reach this emotional content in moments of sudden relaxation that follow 'intense' conditions of 'steady observation'. In such a state, he argued, 'any beautiful, any impressive visual object, or collection of objects, falling upon the eye, is carried to the heart with a power not known under other circumstances'.[9] His poetry allows for this sense of vivid realization by engaging our concentration and then abruptly breaking it with an image or noise, such as the screams of the owls in 'There Was a Boy' (1798). Like the Danish boy, the boy of Winander, whether living or dead, seems woven into the natural world. Both poems affect us through their somatic as much as their conceptual meaning, the boy of Winander's 'mimic hootings' (10) an imitation of language that holds more meaning than the narrator's words, encouraging the reader to listen as much as look at the poem. After all, it can be hard to see the vaporous wanderers in these poems, stripped as they are of material being and only available to us as echoes of nature.

The boy of Winander teaches us how to hear through the example of his reciprocal communication with the owls. His steady focus on them – praying to the owls with his hands 'Press'd closely palm to palm' (8) – is returned by their 'quivering peals / And long halloos, and screams, and echoes loud / Redoubled and redoubled' (13–15). The poem is also structured by a series of echoes: 'many a time' / 'sometimes', 'along the edges' / 'along that bank', 'would he stand alone' / 'I have stood', 'hung'/ 'hangs'. But it is the silence that follows the boy's interaction with the owls that carries the sound of nature 'far into his heart' (20), a sense of stillness that the narrator learns to imitate while standing motionless before the boy's grave, 'listening' (19), like the boy, to nothingness. This abeyance signifies a kind of pause or withdrawal that implies a renunciation of the desire to know or fix meaning, one that is repeated in Wordsworth's many revisions of the poem (in both Book V of *The Prelude* and *Poems*, 1815). By voluntarily letting go of the need to understand, the narrator is granted a sense of peace: he finds freedom in the experience of 'unknowing'. Those who seek to manage or control their existence, by contrast, are denied such freedom, a consequence Wordsworth explores in his poem 'Michael'. As the next section shows, the character of Michael is so desperate to govern and regulate his family's destiny that he ends up both alienating those he loves and also losing the land that connects him to his wider community.

'Michael' and 'The Brothers'

'Michael' is a political pastoral about the shattering impact of industrialization on the livelihood and emotions of a shepherd called Michael, who lives on inherited land with his wife Isabel, son Luke and 'two brave sheep dogs' (93). Their cottage is known as 'the Evening Star' (146) because of the permanent lamplight that shines out from it, its brightness a sign of the family's unremitting labours as they work through each day and night. Michael is almost obsessed with his property and land, but unlike Lucy or the Danish Boy who seem to vanish into nature, he is vividly present on the pasture he owns, living and working on it with a 'stout' (42), 'Intense and frugal' (45) resolve. His relationship with Luke, which is analogous to that between the Old Testament Abraham and Isaac (Genesis 21), is similarly impassioned, their affectionate bond emotionalized by the land on which they work together:

> But soon as Luke, full ten years old, could stand
> Against the mountain blasts, and to the heights,
> Not fearing toil, nor length of weary ways,
> He with his Father daily went, and they
> Were as companions, why should I relate
> That objects which the Shepherd loved before
> Were dearer now? that from the Boy there came

Feelings and emanations, things which were
Light to the sun and music to the wind;
And that the Old Man's heart seemed born again.   (204–13)

The controlled blank verse of this passage, steadied by its reversed biblical syntax ('He with his Father daily went', for example), and reluctant monosyllables ('But soon as Luke, full ten years old, could stand'), is ideally expressive of Michael's deep and heavy feelings for Luke. Compared with the meditative and polysyllabic blank verse of a poem like 'Tintern Abbey', the pace of 'Michael' feels slow, even lethargic, a rhythm that points the reader to the poem's emotionally dense and complex content.

For Wordsworth argued that he had written the poem to show his readers 'that men who do not wear fine cloaths [sic] can feel deeply', but then portrays Michael as a self-involved and distant character who is quite difficult to understand.[10] The poem rests on Michael's decision to send Luke away to work for a merchant in the city in order to pay off his brother's son's debts, incurred due to 'unforeseen misfortunes' (223). On the one hand Michael seems desperately devoted to his family, extended and immediate alike; on the other, he asks Luke to leave the familial home for a life inimical to that of their community, rather than choosing to sell his own land to pay off the debt. Michael is presented as feeling deeply, then, but his emotions are attached to his land and the rural economy. He loves Luke, but overwhelms him with feeling by forcing him to protect the family property with the same sacrificial intensity as he does. When Luke is removed from the land after going to the city, Michael loses his connection with him and invests, not in his son, but in the stone sheep-fold the two planned to build together on the property as a symbol or covenant of their family inheritance.

Critics often condemn the figure of Michael for directing his affections at a crumbling stone pen rather than his son. Yet we might also suggest that Wordsworth presents Michael as a father figure who feels profoundly, almost painfully, for his family, especially his son. Having promised Luke that he will ' "love thee to the last, And bear thy memory with me to the grave" ' (426–7), Michael compulsively visits the sheep-fold as if it were a tomb or sacred site symbolizing his paternal feeling. While Luke disappears from the poem altogether, abruptly falling into 'evil courses' (454) in the city, Michael steps up his daily visits to the 'heap of stones', affectionately attending to it like the biblical Jacob, who gathers a pile of stones as a sign of familial peace (Genesis 31.45). His error, perhaps, is to fail to reflect on and so truly realize his love for Luke by bringing him back home. Instead, he finds consolation in the unfinished sheep-fold, materially useless but aesthetically comforting as a place to ponder 'On man; the heart of man and human life' (33). Like Michael, the reader too might experience such consolation in Wordsworth's language: like the sheep-fold, the poem 'Michael' is unfinished (the story feels curtailed and unevolved), but emotionally reassuring (the poem's form and sound are aesthetically engaging).

By exploring the portrayal of feeling in the poem, readers might, the narrator hopes, become 'my second self when I am gone' (39), enabled, like Wordsworth, by the natural world which continues to grow around Michael's land. Even after Michael's death, the brook that flows beside the 'unfinished Sheepfold' (490) is notably 'boisterous' (491), its rushing movement jolting the poem's otherwise tragic ending into a state of vitality and renewal. The poem's animated ending is foreshadowed throughout the narrative, however, through a series of references to the parables of 'The Lost Sheep', 'The Lost Coin' and 'The Prodigal Son' (Luke 15), all stories that stress the importance of redeeming the lost and marginal through love. 'Michael' also reads like a parable, its plain diction, minimal detail and moral underpinnings giving way to a faith in living affection for nature and community.

The same parable form underlines 'The Brothers', a poem that follows a mariner called Leonard as he visits the graveyard of his 'paternal home' (65) after having spent twenty years at sea. The local Priest, a symbol of institutionalized and so regulated thinking, fails to recognize Leonard, assuming he is a tourist – a 'moping son of Idleness' (11) – who feigns emotion by excessively indulging in 'fancies' (106). Leonard proves, however, that like Michael, he can feel deeply, especially in his heartfelt response to the Priest's recollection of the death of his brother James. A once 'delicate' (327) child with 'the spirit of a mountain-boy' (331), James is presented as a 'boy of Winander' figure, but one who is buried in an unmarked grave. The unmarked grave is significant because it suggests the closeness of the community, one that has 'no need of names and epitaphs' (175). James's real memorial is identified by the Priest as his 'Shepherd's staff' (399), that 'hung – and mouldered' (401) on the rocks from which he fell to his death. Just as Michael finds solace in the land after Luke's departure, so Leonard surrenders his memory of his brother to the natural world where he died, his 'Tears rushing in' and he leaves 'the spot in silence' (403). Like Wordsworth's brother John, Leonard is transformed here into a silent poet, but one who, rather than drowning, lives on to reflect on his feelings as 'A Seaman, a grey headed Mariner' (430).

'The Solitary Reaper' and 'The White Doe of Rylstone'

Wordsworth continued to be drawn to figures living in quiet retreat from the world, leech gatherers, mourning mothers, blind highland boys, gypsies and beggars all providing vehicles through which readers might emotionally and imaginatively confront their own grief and sorrow. He also focused on small and unassuming particulars of the natural world – butterflies, linnets, cuckoos, glow-worms, hedgehogs, robins, celandines, daisies and skylarks – subjects that yielded a lighter lyric that nonetheless associated deep feeling with common subjects. The contemporary reception of these poems was extremely negative, however, reviewers finding *Poems, in Two Volumes* (1807) 'nauseous' and 'puerile', judgements that foreshadowed a modern discomfort with Wordsworth's more vulnerable lyrics.[11]

Yet as Wordsworth reminded readers in his 'Essay, Supplementary to the Preface' (1815), his poetry demands 'to be comprehended *as a study*' (*PW*, III.62); he insisted that all of his poetry, including his minor verses, should be discerned and reflected on. In 'There Was a Boy' and 'To a Butterfly' (1802), he even invokes the 'half-hour' as a unit of meditative time. Only those willing to carefully read his poetry by entraining themselves into it through a 'range' of 'passions' (*PW*, III.64) are open to being animated and moved by the 'wandering Voice' of the cuckoo, the gleam of the sparrow's bright 'blue eggs', the 'Singing, singing' of the skylark, the airy 'Presence' of the linnet or the modesty of the 'Little, humble Celandine'.[12]

The specificity of nature, Wordsworth suggests, practises our senses to see and hear the world in a way that brings us both closer to it and to those within it, an idea he explored in 'The Solitary Reaper'. Wordsworth's description of a female harvester singing to herself as she works achieves this by at once evoking nature (in references to the vale and the sea), Dorothy (the first line echoes her prose sketch of the reapers she saw with her brother on their Scottish tour) and the poet's friend, Thomas Wilkinson (whose draft account of a tour in Scotland alluded to a 'Female who was reaping alone' and singing in 'the sweetest human voice I ever heard').[13] The poem also sets up the narrator as a model listener, vigilantly engaged in her ambient song and commanding readers to do the same:

> Behold her, single in the field,
> Yon solitary Highland Lass!
> Reaping and singing by herself;
> Stop here, or gently pass!
> Alone she cuts, and binds the grain,
> And sings a melancholy strain;
> O listen! for the Vale profound
> Is overflowing with the sound.   (1–8)

On one level, the poem alerts readers to her social condition: she is a young girl alone in a cornfield relentlessly labouring and singing sorrowfully to give her work rhythm and keep herself company. Yet the overflow of her song immerses the narrator, who hears the melody at an interior and emotional level. He might be blocked from the content of its meaning by linguistic and vernacular boundaries ('Will no one tell me what she sings?' he asks in line 17), but he is also seduced by the sub-textual sounds and rhythms of its tune and the way in which the reaper embodies the song's refrain. Whatever detains the narrator to 'Stop here' and 'listen!' is not simply the words of her song, but the somatic pattern of her body and voice. The two are connected aurally, 'I saw her sing*ing* at her work, / And o'er the sickle bend*ing*' (27–8), and rhythmically, as her singing and bending tune us into an almost spiritual state. The echo of Psalm 126.5 ('they that sow in tears shall reap in joy') throughout the ballad suggests that her song is also redemptive, both for herself and for those who stop and think as they listen. It is as if Wordsworth refuses to let anything intrude into the scene – no nightingale (9), no cuckoo (14) – so that the 'sweeter' (13) tone of her voice might excite readers into a kind of trance. Now spellbound, readers feel temporarily separated from their surroundings, the meaning of the poem and the consolation of nature, and are thus liberated to reawaken into a vitalized condition of sensual awareness.

For Wordsworth, this process is enabled by the imagination, a breaking-in of consciousness that allows him to sense and feel the reaper's 'natural sorrow, loss, or pain' (23) and imagine what he cannot understand. What does signify to him is the habitual emotion embedded in her repeated lyric, one that teaches him to hear feeling:

> I listened till I had my fill:
> And, as I mounted up the hill,
> The music in my heart I bore,
> Long after it was heard no more. (29–32)

While the physical and emotional immediacy of the reaper's song might wane, it remains recognizable to him through intuition and emotion. Wordsworth is not implying that he has memorized the girl's melodic sequences, but rather that he can remember the shape and feel of her song. Such recollection might even be painful, the line 'The music in my heart I bore' hinting that her song is burdensome to him as a reminder both of a broken rural economy, and also of the pressure he feels to understand the world through the imagination (an anxiety that resounds throughout *The Prelude*). Wordsworth transforms this pain into joy by suggesting that self-dependence, solitude and repeated reflection give way to an emotional maturity from which warm communal feeling emerges.

Wordsworth continued to advocate reflective retreat from society in 'The White Doe of Rylstone' (1807–8), the poem he considered 'in conception, the highest work he had ever produced'.[14] While critics are quick to accuse Wordsworth of political heresy in moving to a position of quietude after John's death, he is clear in his 'Essay, Supplementary to the Preface' (1815) how important it is that feeling excite external and internal efforts (*PW*, III.81). As his emotional development repaired and renovated him, enabling active pursuit of political commitments within his community, so his poems begin to invest not in the dispossessed but in those, like Emily Norton in 'The White Doe', who are able to act on their sorrow by converting it into to joy.

'The White Doe of Rylstone' refers to a legend that relates how, after the dissolution of the monasteries, a white doe is said to appear every Sunday in the churchyard of Bolton Priory Abbey, stay for the service and then disappear back to Rylstone, the family seat of the Nortons. Wordsworth relates how Richard Norton and eight of his nine sons are executed during the 'Rising of the North' (1569), a Roman Catholic insurrection that his remaining children, Francis and Emily, refuse to join as a mark of constancy to their dead mother's Protestantism. When the rebellion fails, Francis is killed while dutifully taking his father's rebel banner to St Mary's shrine at Bolton Abbey, and Emily is left alone, forced into a life of contemplation. When Walter Scott pointed out the historical inaccuracies of Wordsworth's portrait, the poet replied that he intended his poem to be loyal, not to history, but to its oral folklore meaning. He reiterated the point to Isabella Fenwick: 'Everything that is attempted by the principal personages in "The White Doe" fails, so far as its object is external and substantial. So far as it is moral & spiritual it succeeds.'[15]

Emily is the most spiritual figure in the poem: Wordsworth described her as a symbol of 'undisturbed humanity' and 'pure etherial [sic] spirituality'.[16] Unlike Michael or Margaret, whose grief and loss are only partly recovered through the sympathetic response of readers, Emily patiently works out how to address her own suffering by engaging with the emotional as well as material being of nature. While she initially seems resigned to a stoicism encouraged by her brother Francis, she soon realizes that to deny emotion is to deny being human, an epiphany signified in the look of 'loving-kindness' (1624) that characterizes her appearance. This epiphany is enabled by the white doe, 'most beautiful, clear-white, / A radiant creature, silver bright!' (1647–8). As the doe looks up at her with its 'its head upon her knee' (1654) and Emily remembers seeing the animal with her family as a child, she is freed to experience the depths (or 'abyss' as Wordsworth calls it in line 1821) of her grief, let go of it, and thus feel her sorrow modulate into love:

> The pleading look the Lady viewed,
> And, by her gushing thoughts subdued,
> She melted into tears –

A flood of tears, that flowed apace,
Upon the happy Creature's face.
Oh, moment ever blest! O Pair
Beloved of Heaven, Heaven's chosen care.   (1660–6)

Still grieving for his own brother, Wordsworth creates in Emily a mourner able to accept her loss and transform it into joy through her readiness to relate to a gentle and redemptive envoy of nature (the doe is noticeably distinct from the furiously stormy part of nature that destroyed John and his ship). At the same time, the poem reiterates Wordsworth's belief in the fixed relationship of love between humanity and nature, the doe able to humanize Emily only because she responds to its advances with affection.

The Prelude

The Prelude is Wordsworth's semi-autobiographical account of how he comes to understand himself through a relationship with nature. During the course of the poem, he learns that his mind and imagination are awakened, not by intellectual pursuits, but by emotions and sympathies to which he is led by nature. The narrator thus concludes: 'From Nature doth emotion come' (XII.1). If Wordsworth uses the poem to suggest that emotion, fleeting and unpredictable, structures life, then it follows that his reported experience of existence will be coloured by uncertainty and chance. Part of the poem's achievement is to show the reader that life does not make coherent 'sense', and that we learn most from reflecting on accidental and random moments that reveal more to us than that which we plan or expect.

For example, in Book VI, Wordsworth recounts crossing the Alps with his friend Robert Jones, a journey he expected would grant him a sublime experience in which he might confront nature in all its vastness and achieve heightened consciousness. En route, however, he gets lost in the Simplon Pass, and realizes that he has missed the experience he sought by unknowingly passing through the mountain range (VI.506–24). Briefly stunned by disappointment, he turns to the 'Imagination!' (VI.525) as a compensatory experience and finds that it gives him the emotional high he wanted, revealing 'The invisible world' (VI.536) in a moment of quick '"glory"' (VI.532). Yet this experience gives way to something even deeper and unforeseen in the following lines. Suddenly, Wordsworth hears the rocks and crags mutter to him that the profound feeling he desires is always already there in the everyday details of nature: the sky, the wind, the woods, waterfalls, blossoms, trees, sunlight, stones. He calls these things the 'Characters of the great Apocalypse' (VI.570), because together they tell him what feeling and consciousness really is – shared and particular (in the details of nature and with his friend Jones), not private and abstract (in isolated moments of sublimity):

> The immeasurable height
> Of woods decaying, never to be decayed,
> The stationary blasts of water-falls,
> And every where along the hollow rent
> Winds thwarting winds, bewildered and forlorn,
> The torrents shooting from the clear blue sky,
> The rocks that muttered close upon our ears,
> Black drizzling crags that spake by the way-side
> As if a voice were in them, the sick sight
> And giddy prospect of the raving stream,
> The unfettered clouds and region of the heavens,
> Tumult and peace, the darkness and the light
> Were all like workings of one mind, the features
> Of the same face, blossoms upon one tree,
> Characters of the great Apocalypse,
> The types and symbols of Eternity,
> Of first and last, and midst, and without end.   (VI.556–72)

As the landscape speaks to him here, he feels the 'living voice' of nature, one that constantly shifts and redefines itself through human interaction, as opposed to the dead voice of the allegorizing classical literature he read at Cambridge.

Wordsworth's 'apocalypse' (he only uses the word once in his poetry) is individual and personal here: it is a moment of revelation that the poet might remember in different ways at different times, rather than an event with a fixed or logical meaning. He is not transformed by what he sees at the Simplon Pass, nor does nature reveal some eternal truth to him: instead, he recognizes that truth is partial, splintered and 'without end', always changing, like the meaning of language itself. The word 'characters', for example, refers both to the aspects of nature that populate the Simplon Pass, and also to written characters, or letters, which, like nature, own the potential to create meanings that are dark and frightening, as well as light and joyful.

Wordsworth makes the same connection between nature and writing earlier in *The Prelude*, recalling in Book I how, after ice-skating with a group of children on Esthwaite, he retires into a 'silent bay' (I.475) to contemplate the night sky and the 'shadowy banks' (I.480) by which he is surrounded. As in the Simplon Pass, the world makes him dizzy, rolling around him with 'visible motion' (I.486). As he watches, however, all becomes 'tranquil as a dreamless sleep' (I.489), moving him to ask the 'Presences of Nature' (I.490) if they will always be with him. Will they, he inquires, continue to perform that secret 'ministry' (I.494) that reveals to humans the uncertainty and fragility of meaning by impressing 'upon all forms the characters / Of danger or desire' (I.497–8)? Deciding to 'pursue this theme through every change' (I.502), Wordsworth commits himself to exploring this question, and writes *The Prelude* to do so by thinking about how nature helps us live with the arbitrary quality of existence and meaning.

The multiple editions and revisions that exist of *The Prelude* exemplify Wordsworth's refusal to understand life as coherent or systematic. A two-part version was completed in 1799, a five-book copy by 1804, thirteen books by 1805, constant revisions until 1839, and published by Wordsworth's wife Mary after his death as the 1850 fourteen-book *The Prelude*. In line with much modern criticism, this book quotes from the 1805 edition, considered more politically and emotionally raw than the later 1850 copy, which is thought to present the same incidents and events but from a more orthodox religious and social perspective. Even though the poem was not published in Wordsworth's lifetime, readers of *The Excursion*'s 'Preface' were aware that the poet had promised a grand poetic 'review of his own mind' in which he would 'examine how far Nature and Education had qualified him' to write an epic for modern times (*PW*, III.5). This longer work, tasked to him by Coleridge, was to be a humanized Miltonic epic called *The Recluse; or Views of Nature, Man, and Society*. While some of Parts I and II were completed ('Home at Grasmere', 'The Tuft of Primroses' and *The Excursion*), Part III was never written, and Wordsworth spent his life writing and revising the introduction, which he called 'The Poem to Coleridge' or 'The Growth of a Poet's Mind'.

As an unfinished poem (literally and symbolically), *The Prelude* can be difficult to read, perpetually reminding its reader that the condition of being human is splintered and fragmented (the poet declares that when he thinks about himself he feels split apart into 'Two consciousnesses, conscious of myself / And of some other Being', II.32–3). Yet it is the poem's messiness and disconcerting lack of unity that helps communicate its exploration of the self as a psychological and emotional complex that resists linguistic definition. The various relationships through which Wordsworth understands this self – to nature, the imagination, memory and political consciousness – form the scaffold of its narrative, which traces Wordsworth's memories of childhood and school-time, those alienating terms at Cambridge, the vacation tour with Jones, residences in London and revolutionary France and finally of his emotional restoration via nature, the imagination and love of his friends in the Lake District.

Wordsworth presents nature as a teacher in *The Prelude*, one that shows him how to love others by preparing him for those emotions – sad and joyful – that follow from human relationships. His experience of nature is depicted as both material, providing him with a 'real solid world' of 'gentle airs, / Birds, running streams, and hills so beautiful / On golden evenings'; and also spiritual, this same scene appearing to him as one breathed across by a ghostly 'charcoal Pile' of smoke (VIII.604, 619–23). Similarly, Wordsworth's sense-based connection with nature physically vitalizes him into a state of controlled passion in which he is then enabled to imagine the consequent sensations through personal vision. He might feel the 'loud dry wind / Blow through my ears!' for example, but it reverberates with a 'strange utterance' only he hears (I.348–9). When he looks up at a 'lovely Tree / Beneath a frosty moon', it casts a 'fairy' light onto the scene that illuminates 'tranquil visions' of 'human Forms and superhuman Powers' only he sees (VI.101–9).

Enraptured by the 'spells' (III.232) of nature, Wordsworth often feels that he transcends his senses in *The Prelude*, 'soothed by a sense of touch / From the warm ground, that balanced me, else lost / Entirely, seeing nought, nought hearing' (I.89–91). Only when 'an acorn from the trees / Fell audibly, and with a startling sound' (I.93–4) is the poet retuned to the physical world, but even this description amplifies the drop of the falling seed, conveying its epiphanic intensity. Nature grants Wordsworth these epiphanies because it works in relation with his imagination, granting him access to his inner self in relation to the natural world. This kind of imagination is productive, rather than reproductive, inventing the world anew by dissolving and then recreating it, as opposed to replicating or memorizing its qualities and reproducing them in a fixed form (an alternative mental faculty Coleridge called 'fancy').[17]

Wordsworth privileged the imagination (rather than logic or rationality) because it facilitated spontaneous and so 'natural' ways of learning, thinking and perceiving that embody the 'wiser Spirit' of 'unreasoning progress' (V.384–5). The philosopher Paul de Man famously suggests that Wordsworth's conception of the imagination threatens to annihilate the real world, leaving us only with a kind of nothingness.[18] We might argue that this 'nothingness' is apparent in the Arab dream episode of Book V, which relates a dreamed encounter between a man and a desert-bound Bedouin holding a stone and a shell. As the stone transmutes into a dry mathematical textbook (Euclid's *Elements*, V.88), the shell issues a 'loud prophetic blast of harmony' that foretells destruction and death in the form of an impassioned ode (V.96). As an exaggerated poet figure, 'crazed / By love and feeling and internal thought' (V.144–5), the Arab serves to warn Wordsworth and his readers against becoming absorbed in any form of language, mathematical, scientific or poetic. But rather than falling into the 'abyss' of endless signification, that is, Paul de Man's 'nothingness', Wordsworth turns back to 'Nature's self' (V.230). He inserts the boy of Winander passage ('There Was a Boy') into *The Prelude* as a model of emotional experience (V.389–422) and then reinvests in that 'heart-experience' of 'raw' nature – the 'woods and fields' – to anchor him back in the world (V.609–13).

Wordsworth's resolve to remain true to nature is tested throughout *The Prelude*, especially by his experiences in France and London. When he visits London in Book VII, for example, he is psychologically overwhelmed by the city, paralysed by the rapid rhythm of life there, as well as the intense and unexpected sensory stimulation of discontinuous and forever changing images and impressions. He finds the spectacle of London's annual summer carnival, St Bartholomew's Fair, 'a hell / For eyes and ears!' (VII.659–60), describing it as a microcosm of the larger city that is horrifically alive with mistreated slaves, abused animals and monstrous performers, 'Grimacing, writhing, screaming' (VII.673). Frozen in what he calls 'blank confusion!' (VII.696) before the scene, Wordsworth remains lost in London's 'overflowing streets' where 'the face of every one / That passes by me is a mystery' (VII.595, 597–8).

While rural society feels social and communal to him, city life appears to shut down human relationships, marked as they are by the profound isolation captured in the figure of the blind beggar, abandoned and alone and 'propped against a Wall' (VII.613). The beggar wears an epitaph-like 'written paper' pinned to his chest 'to explain / The story of the Man, and who he was' (VII.614–15), and yet Wordsworth refrains from relating his story because it is abstract and unintelligible, disconnected from the interpersonal context that would grant it meaning. The words on his label substitute rather than express meaning, and the beggar appears in the poem as an immutable figure of loneliness and specular isolation that serves to intensify Wordsworth's alienation, severing him from his own self: 'And all the ballast of familiar life, / The present, and the past; hope, fear; all stays, / All laws of acting, thinking, speaking man / Went from me' (VII.604–7).

The wintry tone of Book VII only mellows once Wordsworth returns to the social world of nature, where he reconnects with himself by relating to others. He facilitates this process by drawing on what he terms 'spots of time', specific memories charged with feeling that when recalled serve to cushion painful experience. Wordsworth's own spots of time – snaring woodcocks (I.318), stealing a boat (I.373), sailing on Windermere (II.57), visiting Furness Abbey (II.110), encountering a drowned man (V.470), realizing Robespierre was dead (X.535), seeing a mouldered gibbet mast (XI.291), hearing his father had died (XII.366) – are all primary or climactic moments that stir the self back into his or her present moment. Wordsworth suggests that many spots of time can be recovered from childhood, but he is equally insistent that they are instants of our 'first childhood' (XI.276), that is, moments from any period of life wherein we first feel an emotion or experience a new aspect of the world:

> There are in our existence spots of time,
> Which with distinct pre-eminence retain
> A renovating Virtue, whence, depressed
> By false opinion and contentious thought,
> Or aught of heavier or more deadly weight
> In trivial occupations, and the round
> Of ordinary intercourse, our minds
> Are nourished and invisibly repaired;
> A virtue by which pleasure is enhanced,
> That penetrates, enables us to mount
> When high, more high, and lifts us up when fallen.   (XI.258–68)

The biblical association of 'lifts us up' (see, for example, Psalm 121.1, Ecclesiastes 4.10, and Mark 9.27) is suggestive of the absolving quality of the spot of time, experiences that, while not always positive, are infused with the 'deepest feeling' (XI.271), one that which we must experience rather than 'judge' (XI.238). This is why Wordsworth declares that memory is not a nostalgic faculty, but one that allows us to reflect on our immediate moment: ' "Be it so, / It is an injury", said I, "to this day / To think of any thing but present joy" ' (I.107–9).

By developing an awareness of the present, the poet implies, one always has the potential to access joy, even if this must necessarily emerge from painful feelings. In 'Surprised by Joy', for example, Wordsworth's sonnet on the death of his daughter, Catherine, the narrator suggests joy can be a shocking experience, fleetingly intruding into sorrow. His emotional vulnerability to grief and joy in the sonnet is reiterated at the end of *The Prelude*, where Wordsworth reflects on how quickly our emotions change and how life itself comprises an indeterminate, interrupted and incomplete experience. Having climbed to the summit of Snowdon, Wordsworth ascends into a moonlit scene of misty clouds to see a 'blue chasm; a fracture in the vapour, / A deep and gloomy breathing-place' and 'roaring with one voice' (XIII.56–9). Meditating 'Upon the lonely Mountain when the scene / Had passed away' (XIII.67–8), the poet reflects on the vision, wondering whether he has witnessed the 'sense of God' (XIII.72), the sublimity of nature (XIII.85), or the strength of his own sensory or imaginative abilities. As the vision fades, however, he is returned to the 'face of human life' (XIII.181): his physical self, Jones who travels with him and finally Coleridge (XIII.442). That Wordsworth chooses to end the poem with an allusion to Coleridge, a fellow prophet of nature and love, intimates that his final investment is in a communal model of human dependence and friendship.

The Excursion

The humanized and communal close of *The Prelude* suggests that Words-worth moved from an exploration of self-identity towards a social model of subjectivity that he developed more fully in his longest published poem, *The Excursion* (initially intended to be a section of *The Recluse*). Begun in 1798 and published in 1814, the poem was famously hated by Romantic critics but much loved by the Victorians, who found its biblical language and religious consolation comforting and familiar. Unlike the poet-narrator of *The Prelude*, the poet-narrator of *The Excursion* defers much of his narrative authority to his travelling companions – the Wanderer, the Pastor and the Solitary – choos-ing, in silent-poet mode, to record their reflections rather than highlight his own. The poetic vocation thus becomes a practical rather than an introspec-tive one, serving to expedite the means (a poem) for others to express their thoughts and feelings (by creating a space for his companions to speak and for readers of the poem to reflect). Self-analytic modes of expression, then, such as spots of time or rhetorical addresses to abstract ideas, are replaced by communal story-telling, and the only speech we hear is that of the Pastor to his flock (living and dead) in the ninth and final book of the poem.

Many critics read *The Excursion* not as a story or religious allegory, but as a public commentary on contemporary historical events. War is berated in Book I; the failure of the French Revolution haunts Book III; the moral responsibil-ity the state and Church of England owe to the nation is discussed in Book VI; the destruction of rural England by industrialization and manufacture is attacked in Book VIII; and Book IX includes an appeal to the government to provide a national education system. Yet even these references to history are given particular, rather than general meaning, the Wanderer, Solitary, Pastor and Poet each working to engage the reader in their own memories of these events to communalize them as shared memories on which a nation of readers might draw. As in *The Prelude*, however, memory is displaced in *The Excursion* to privilege present feeling or 'independent happiness', experienced 'Not as a refuge from distress or pain, / A breathing-time, vacation, or a truce, / But for its absolute self; a life of peace' (III.390–2).

Like many of Wordsworth's readers, the Solitary seeks but cannot feel such peace. He is blocked from emotion because of his disconnection from both his own self and his community, emotionally paralysed following the death of his wife and children. Yet his disillusionment provides the sceptical reader with a companion in the poem, a figure who might initially, with the reader, find the lengthy perorations of the Wanderer and Pastor difficult or dry. He also shows the reader where to find recovery, not in a moment of great revelation or epiphany, but in the shared journey he takes through the valley to the Pastor's parish with his 'gentle Friends' (III.609). The 'air of open fellowship' (II.932) he finds with the three men offers 'succour' (IV.1083), 'domestic love' (V.57) and a renewed relationship with nature that individual insight cannot offer.

Nature is central to *The Excursion*, not only because it provides the poem's topography but also because it is transformed into a spiritualized site of solace that effects real change on the travellers. The story of 'The Ruined Cottage', for example, related in Book I by the Wanderer (a revised Pedlar figure), becomes a cautionary tale about the effects of disengaging with the natural world, Margaret isolating herself within a sterile depression even as nature grows up around her cottage. The Solitary, by contrast, clearly articulates his sorrow, recalling the deaths of his family, departure for America and disappointed return to England devoid of faith in religion or humanity. He also allows others to release him from this sorrow, not by asking them to fix the immediate situation, but by absorbing his distress through an intimacy and attention learned from nature. Sustained redemption, the Wanderer and Pastor insist, is only offered by nature, an ' "active principle" ' (IX.3) of solace and revitalization that renews feeling to those prepared to enter into it:

> – For the Man,
> Who, in this spirit, communes with the Forms
> Of Nature, who with understanding heart,
> Doth know and love, such Objects as excite
> No morbid passions, no disquietude,
> No vengeance, and no hatred – needs must feel
> The joy of that pure principle of love
> So deeply, that, unsatisfied with aught
> Less pure and exquisite, he cannot choose
> But seek for objects of a kindred love
> In Fellow-natures, and a kindred joy.   (IV.1201–11)

Not only does this willingness to yield to 'Nature's humbler power' (IV.1184) offer a template of relation that enables affectionate interaction between people, but it also reduces stress (the lover of nature will perceive 'His feelings of aversion softened down', IV.1213) and connects him to a 'holy tenderness' (IV.1214) absent from organized religions. For nature's 'inarticulate language' (IV.1201) speaks to the men in a way God cannot, divinity expressed not in church ceremonial or doctrinal law, but in the 'impulse and utterance' of the 'whispering Air' (IV.1164) across 'fertile fields', 'shadowy' vales and waving 'woods' (IX.742–4). The poem shapes nature as a space where religious sensibilities, Christian or otherwise, can function, preached by the Pastor in open-air sermons bounded by the mountains and valleys. The physical space of the Pastor's Church is thus dominated by a memorial sundial, a pagan and aesthetic object 'For public use' (VI.514), serving to connect parishioners with each other, rather than with ecclesial authority or a proscribed notion of God: 'human anthems' (IV.1157) replace religious ones, as friendship replaces normative familial ties.

Indeed the Wanderer, unmarried and childless, argues for a collective model of domestic affection that overrides biological, geographical or class limitations. When we finally arrive at the Pastor's household, for example, his son's friendship with another boy is privileged over exclusive inter-familial bonds, the two 'Not Brothers they in feature or attire, / But fond Companions' (VIII.555–6) and 'Blest in their several and their common lot!' (IX.257). Where the boy of Winander seems absorbed into nature, the two boys here find joy in each other within a natural landscape, one that also frames the communal picnic that closes the poem. The travellers remain in sight of the church (IX.575), but sit on 'mossy' (IX.581) stones, 'admiring quietly / The frame and general aspect of the scene' (IX.582–3). This final apocalyptic vision – 'rays of light' shooting 'upwards' into the 'blue firmament' and oozing like liquid fire through the 'thin ethereal mould' of 'little floating clouds' (IX.592–608) – imagines a 'unity sublime!' that reworks the ending of *The Prelude*. Here the vision is shared, integrating not only the material world with a spiritual one, but joining the lives of the companions through communal response and feeling.

Late poems

The note of resolution on which *The Excursion* ends, however, fails to persuade many readers, and William Hazlitt is not alone in thinking the poem feels 'stillborn from the press'.[19] For most modern critics *The Excursion* marks the end of Wordsworth's 'great' poetry, and his later work is often only deemed useful as a way of measuring the pre-eminence of the former work. Yet Wordsworth was always insistent in his early lyrics that good poetry exposes passions and feelings anchored in 'permanent forms of nature', a bedrock that by the early nineteenth century had been desecrated by industrialization. Wordsworth perhaps could have chosen to continue writing poems about nature and politics in a similar aesthetic mode. He chose instead, however, to write essays and letters about the destruction of the environment and rural communities, focusing his poetic concerns on more sage-like poems, like *The Excursion, The River Duddon: A Series of Sonnets* (1820) and the *Ecclesiastical Sketches* (1837).

The most notable difference between these poems and the earlier work is Wordsworth's style. Where his narrating voice is initially emotionally open, frenetic, eerie and unsettled, it becomes rigid, stately, classicized and conventional in the later poetry. *The River Duddon* sonnet series, for example, evokes many of the same scenes and images conjured in the *Lyrical Ballads*. The narrator, like Wordsworth's early speakers, stresses the visionary beauty of the river as it flows from Wrynose Fell to the sea (sonnets IV and V) and hears its low 'whisper' (sonnet XXI.1); invokes the strength of traditional rural community while warning of the damage tourists and visitors might effect on the landscape (in the opening dedication and sonnet XXIII); and singles out individuals as emblems of shared feeling, harmoniously working with the land and spiritually guiding those who live there (in the Michael-like figure of Reverend Robert Walker, championed in the footnote to sonnet XVII).

Yet the *River Duddon* sonnets are perhaps too polished, formally dedicated to his brother Christopher, who, as an ordained Cambridge don, was the very embodiment of orthodoxy. Its diction, style and tone also bar the edgy awkwardness of poems like 'The Thorn' or 'The Idiot Boy', verses that snag our feelings and effectively, if uncomfortably, pull on them. The sequence is preoccupied, then, not with Wordsworth's emotional response to the scenes evoked, but with his longstanding topographical knowledge of them, inviting in readers to whom his earlier poetry seemed disturbed and senseless. Even later balladic poems like 'The Gleaner' (1828), 'A Wren's Nest' (1833), 'The Labourer's Noon-Day Hymn' (1834), 'Grace Darling' (1843) or 'The Westmoreland Girl' (1845) are intent on the versification of occurrence and event at the expense of emotional impact. Wordsworth had become a laureate to the early Victorians rather than a teacher of feeling.

In 'Laodamia' (1814), for example, Wordsworth returned to one of his often-explored themes: the suffering that accompanies mourning. In this poem, however, the narrator appears to sentimentalize Laodamia's grief, packaging it within stylized classical references, and erasing any of the raw sorrow that such figures as Martha Ray or Lucy Gray's parents endure. Laodamia, wife of Protesilaus, is doubly bereaved after begging Zeus to animate a statue of her husband that becomes only momentarily alive, like the emotion within the poem itself. She is almost punished for the 'wilful' feeling (159) that causes her demise, and even after death, Laodamia is exiled from 'blissful quiet' to a state of apparent eternal misery ''mid unfading bowers' (163). Her fate is bluntly declared by Wordsworth, Laodamia's unmistakable death divested of any of the cryptic thrill of Lucy's intermediary existence.

'The Norman Boy' (1840–2) too appears like a pale reflection of 'The Danish Boy', living, like his earlier counterpart, with nature and his sheep in a small hut made of 'branches rent and withered and decayed' (13). Yet the Norman Boy has none of the ghostly magnetism of the Danish prince. He is presented to us not by a hypnotized observer, but by a poet who repeats the story as given to him 'from an English Dame' (5) who is interested in the boy as a model of Christian piety. The tale focuses on the boy's homespun cross, 'wrought' by him from 'limber twigs' (18–19) and 'engrafted on the top of his small edifice' (20) as a 'standard for the true / And faithful service of his heart' (25–6). The symbolism of the cross is glaring, and looks towards a sequel ('The Poet's Dream') that focuses even more piously on a vision of 'the Norman Boy kneeling alone in prayer' (8).

The Christianizing project of Wordsworth's later career is also apparent in his poetic revisions. He rewrote 'Salisbury Plain' as the more morally transparent 'Guilt and Sorrow', concluding it with the murderer full of contrition before God as he is hanged for his crime; and replaced *The Prelude*'s paganism with a revisionary Anglicanism. Revisiting the Simplon Pass in sonnet XXX of 'Memorials of a Tour on the Continent, 1820', Wordsworth seems to have lapsed from the intensity of *The Prelude* into a wistful disquiet, blocked from the 'One life' that rolls through all earthly things and forced to reluctantly turn to the next world. In the 'Vernal Ode' (1817), for example, Wordsworth sees nature, not as a 'lover of the meadows and the woods', but as a sage, perceiving the world through a 'spiritual eye / That aids or supersedes our grosser sight' (3–4). Nature is no longer 'deeply interfused' within the poet's sensory and immediate being, then, but is instead perceived as a sign of future redemption, the 'earth and stars' signifying only as forms of nature that compose 'a universal heaven!' (125).

Critical reception

Since the publication of the *Lyrical Ballads*, critics have sought to interpret, decode, unravel, mythologize and attack Wordsworth's poetry and prose. While early critics seemed uncertain about his poetry, the Victorians regarded Wordsworth's voice as confident and prophetic, a view dismantled by modern critics who prefer to read his poetry as anxious or deliberately imprecise. As Wordsworth reminds us, however, thinking is never linear or chronological, and the critical reception of his work can only be suggestively demarcated, biographic work blurring into phenomenological and psychological readings, as political and historicist interpretation catalyse the new prosody and ethical criticism. Modern readers have the advantage of drawing on the now complete Cornell edition as well as numerous searchable electronic databases, and yet, as the variety of readings discussed here attest, Wordsworth's work is notoriously difficult to label.

The uncertain meaning of this work, however, lends it an absorbing fragility that demands a reflective and attentive criticism: as Geoffrey Hartman asserts, we 'understand Wordsworth best when we are too near ourselves, too naked in our self-consciousness.'[1] Biographical explorations of Wordsworth by Mary Moorman, Stephen Gill, Juliet Barker, Keith Hanley and Duncan Wu (and of his sister by Pamela Woof and Frances Wilson) offer us several routes into the poet's life, and critics like Lucy Newlyn highlight the complexities inherent in Wordsworth's psychological being.[2] Where some readers, like Bernard Groom, find patterns and unity in the poetry, others such as Frances Ferguson see a flawed, complex and vulnerable writer.[3] However critics choose to portray Wordsworth, and there are certainly a vast number of interpretations of him available, he still attracts a devoted and engaged readership, one founded by the Victorians.

Victorian consolation

John Stuart Mill claimed that Wordsworth's poetry had rescued him from a deep depression, an 'oblivion', he wrote in his *Autobiography* (1873), that threatened to overwhelm him. Mill turned in vain to his 'favourite books', but found that they expressed a 'state of mind' 'too like my own', tense and apprehensive. Wordsworth's poems, however, served as 'a medicine', a source of 'inward joy, of sympathetic and imaginative pleasure, which could be shared in by all human beings'. 'There have certainly been … greater poets than Wordsworth', wrote Mill,

> but poetry of deeper and loftier feeling could not have done for me at that time what his did. I needed to be made to feel that there was real, permanent happiness in tranquil contemplation. Wordsworth taught me this, not only without turning away from, but with a greatly increased interest in the common feelings and common destiny of human beings.[4]

His fellow Victorians agreed. Tennyson walked nine miles along the river Wharfe to Bolton Abbey, half hoping for a glimpse of the white doe; Felicia Hemans crowned Wordsworth the 'moral', 'intellectual' and spiritual guide of the nineteenth century; Elizabeth Gaskell urged visitors to the Lake District not to leave without a copy of Wordsworth's complete works; the moral philosopher William Knight dedicated his life to editing Wordsworth's work; George Eliot, Elizabeth Barrett Browning and Adelaide Anne Procter revered both his poetry and theories of emotion; and countless writers introduce their own works with epigraphs from his poetry and prose.[5] The late Victorian critic Henry Hudson ranked him 'as the most spiritual and the most spiritualizing of all the English poets, not Shakespeare, no, nor even Milton, excepted: indeed, so far as I know or believe, the world has no poetry outside the Bible that can stand a comparison with his in this respect'.[6] As Stephen Gill remarks, the correspondence files at the Wordsworth Library are filled with letters from readers intent on expressing their gratitude to a poet to whom they invariably turned for instruction and whose home at Rydal Mount they treated like a shrine. Wordsworth's 'wish to be considered as a Teacher, or as nothing' seemed to have found fulfilment by the 1840s.[7]

The Victorians, then, did not recognize William Blake's 'Heathen Philosopher' who rose 'up against the Spiritual Man', nor Francis Jeffrey's subversive and vulgar poet, nor William Hazlitt's 'God of his own idolatry'.[8] Where Mill saw a consolatory poet, Matthew Arnold too found a spiritual guide, Wordsworth drawing his power from the environment, thought Arnold, rather than God: 'Nature herself seems, I say, to take the pen out of his hand, and to write for him with her own bare, sheer, penetrating power.'[9] Like Hemans, John Keble upheld a Christianized and near-saintly image of Wordsworth, arguing that his poetry formed the foundations of a radical humanism that demanded rights for the underprivileged and disenfranchised.[10] Wordsworth seemed to offer the period a steadying hand, one that even Algernon Swinburne admitted 'held more gentle yet more sovereign rule' over readers by invoking the restorative powers of meditation and sympathy. At the same time, Swinburne was wary of the poet's devoted, and, he thought, indulgent disciples, mocking Arnold for thinking 'the dissonant doggerel of Wordsworth's halting lines to a skylark equal or superior to Shelley's incomparable transfusion from notes into words of the spirit of the skylark's song.'[11]

Where Swinburne heard halting rhythms, most Victorians perceived a reserved and regulated quality in Wordsworth's verse that they deeply admired. For John Ruskin, this quality was expressive of the poet's 'grand, consistent, perfectly disciplined, all grasping intellect', so 'majestic in the equanimity of its benevolence – intense as a white fire with chastised feeling.'[12] Thus where Dora Greenwell could look to Wordsworth as a model of 'temperance, industry, courtesy, honesty', Gerard Manley Hopkins felt his poetry like a shock inside his body, 'his insight' into human nature leaving Hopkins all 'in a tremble.'[13]

Like the Bible, from which the poet borrowed both narratives and rhythms, Wordsworth's poetry offered a habitual reading experience that evoked deep feeling about everyday observations. His poems felt familiar, as the aesthete Walter Pater noted, because they presented the reader with an intimate landscape in which the individual can connect 'the stones and trees of a particular spot of earth with the great events of life, till the low walls, the green mounds, the half-obliterated epitaphs' seem 'full of voices.'[14] As this pastoral fantasy became increasingly untenable, however, the spell of Wordsworth's poetry was recast, if not broken, by a newly professionalized generation of critics intent on elevating rigorous close analysis of literary texts over and above hagiographic veneration.

New criticism and phenomenology

A. C. Bradley sustained the Victorian's belletristic approach to Wordsworth's poetry into the following era, and like Hopkins, thought it capable of producing 'a "shock of mild surprise"' in readers. Wordsworth's vision of morality and goodness, Bradley argued, was 'perhaps "slow to begin"', but once one had absorbed it, its impact was '"never ending"', eventually becoming 'twined around the roots' of one's 'being'.[15] By the beginning of the twentieth century, however, Wordsworth's revered image was under attack from critics intent on reading his poetry through conjectural references to lurid biographical details made current by writers such as G. M. Harper and Emile Legouis.[16] Herbert Read too suggested that all of Wordsworth's poetry and biography subsequent to 1792 could be explained away through his feelings of guilt after deserting Annette Vallon; while F. W. Bateson insisted that the troubled and anxious quality of Wordsworth's poetry derived from his not entirely unconscious incestuous feeling for Dorothy.[17]

While such readings at least served to sexualize a poet previously mythologized as chastely untouchable, they were soon out of date. The rise of 'new criticism' in the 1930s and 1940s insisted that all external contexts – biography and history alike – should be overturned in favour of a rigorous form of close reading. New criticism also precluded subjective emotional assessments of the text, frustrated by subjectively penned essays proclaiming neutrality where ideological agendas flourished. As a result, W. K. Wimsatt and Monroe Beardsley warned critics against judging texts in terms of their personal or emotional impact on readers, arguing that the 'affective fallacy' was a distraction from the objective elucidation of poetic language and form.[18] While most critics conceded that a wholly impartial criticism was impossible, T. S. Eliot and F. R. Leavis specifically championed 'Wordsworth's philosophic verse' as bridging the gap 'between thinking and feeling' that so divided contemporary critics.[19] John Dewey too developed his theory of aesthetic experience from Wordsworth's sense of the imagination as a compass that orientates the individual in everyday life, reproducing the external through the internal as 'art'.[20]

Yet new criticism did serve to initiate a phase of textual analysis that would eventually culminate in the recently completed Cornell edition: Ernest de Selincourt, Helen Darbishire and Enid Welsford's extensive unravelling of Wordsworth's mass of revisions and rewritings (particularly de Selincourt's edition of *The Prelude*) opened the poet's work to a diverse critical readership, as well as to editors-in-waiting like Jonathan Wordsworth, Stephen Gill, John O. Hayden and Duncan Wu.[21] At the same time, critics like Cleanth Brooks and John Jones continued to read Wordsworth's narrators as solitary wanderers, brooding on the moral and aesthetic tensions of life and struggling to translate their emotional and material experience into a linguistic form.[22]

The transition from biographic and formalist criticism into the politicized theoretical models of reading that dominated the 1960s and 1970s was largely enabled by the work of M. H. Abrams and Geoffrey Hartman, which finally put to rest concerns that Wordsworth's poetry was too simple to sustain constant rereading. Abrams' key achievement was to establish Romanticism as a field of serious study, introducing the period's intellectual, philosophical, religious and poetic theories inside a narrative that elevated Wordsworth as 'the first great romantic poet'.[23] Like Hartman, and later Harold Bloom, Abrams read Wordsworth as a theodicean (someone who believes in providence) and apocalyptic poet who envisioned a 'marriage between mind and nature' capable of inaugurating a new, 'holy' and renovated world figured through biblical language and history.[24]

Where Abrams documented these ideas, Hartman animated them, his intensely creative, thoughtful and responsible style forging an aesthetically educative criticism that served to refine readers' powers of perception as they studied his books and essays. For Hartman, literary criticism is a more nuanced and sensitive heir to Matthew Arnold's literature of liberal and imaginative reason, able to repair, rather than simply show compassion for, the 'internal injury or psychic trauma' that Wordsworth intimates is inherent in the human condition.[25] Hartman popularized a 'phenomenological' approach to Wordsworth, that is, one that explores poetry as a series of episodes or incidents ('phenomena') that signify to readers as subjectively felt and understood sensations or experiences. He thus addresses Wordsworth's poems as if they are living organisms into which the critic can momentarily breathe meaning and understanding. Hartman's use of phenomenology also merged into other approaches like 'psychoaesthetics' (the power of poetry to repair human grief) and 'theopoesis' (a form of criticism dense with scriptural and theological subtlety).[26] All of these methodologies imply both intellectual insight and compassion, and Hartman's proposition that 'passion leads to perception' helps him to read Wordsworth as a poet marked by an emotive self-consciousness.[27]

In his own discernment of Wordsworth's 'subtlety of thought, sensory dialectics, verbal choices, intertextual echoes, and complex social concerns', Hartman learns and then teaches his reader how to feel and be startled by the poem's 'auditory intensity' without succumbing to formal or historical methodologies.[28] Receptive to both the happy and anxious sensations that inform Wordsworth's 'modern imagination', he reveals it as a spirit that is 'only gradually humanized' by nature and human relationship, always in danger of falling into solipsism but rescued by the habitual rhythms of everyday life that reproduce the world in terms of joy.[29] While successive critics such as Bloom and Paul de Man read Wordsworth more darkly, their analyses fall within a critical scope created by Hartman, one that ushered in a mass of deconstructive readings as it created critical space for the prosodic, aesthetic and historical pursuits of Christopher Ricks, Jonathan Wordsworth, Stephen Gill and Kenneth Johnston.[30] Hartman's attention to both the phenomenology and theology of Wordsworth's language, form and unfolding human vision has also spurred various religious readings, notably William Ulmer's Christian reclamation of Wordsworth.[31]

Psychoanalysis and feminism

Psychoanalytic and feminist scholarship on Wordsworth are often interrelated. Both are concerned with the impact of the poet's absent mother and his consequent (Freudian) attachment to nature as reflected on in the descriptions of childhood in *The Prelude*. For James Heffernan, Wordsworth's representations of mothers and mother figures, whether real (Ann Tyson and Dorothy) or imagined (Martha Ray, the sailor's mother), are informed by infantile sexual desires; whereas critics like Diane Hoeveler Long and Alan Richardson point to Wordsworth's masculine and sometimes destructive desire to exert control over the feminine.[32] Wordsworth's demolition of a hazel tree in the poem 'Nutting', for example, has been perceived as an act of primary narcissism (Rachel Crawford), a rejection of the pastoral for a new modern poetic spirit (Charles Altieri), a guilty masturbatory fantasy (David Perkins) and a Hegelian dramatization of the master–slave dynamic (Robert Burns Neveldine).[33]

For Mary Jacobus, 'Nutting' unfolds a restless drama, which, like other agitated or even apocalyptic moments in Wordsworth's poetry, shows the poet attempting to streamline his world by negating the feminine, transforming nature into mind, history into text and autobiography into vision. Failing to secure a much-desired 'stable identity', she writes, Wordsworth turns to an 'egotistical sublime' (at the Simplon Pass or Snowdon, for example) for reassurance. His response to the sublime, however, is unease and anxiety, factors Jacobus argues are ignored by 'masculine' critics such as Bloom, Hartman and Johnston. These critics, she suggests, elevate 'strong' intellectual experiences like the sublime, even as Wordsworth's poetry betrays their failure to help him work through psychological and emotional issues.[34]

While these deconstructive psychoanalytic readings position Wordsworth in a troubled power dynamic with his world, critics like Jean Hagstrum emphasize the poet's tender affection for and bodily responsiveness to it, one that produces a poetic energy that shapes his transcendental vision.[35] G. Kim Blank in particular has focused on Wordsworth's strategies for achieving self-understanding by reading him as a 'psychobiographical' writer, his poems direct products of his personality. For Blank, the pattern of themes and poetic responses found in Wordsworth's poetry express the poet's inner life as a series of feelings he experiences, reflects on and then leaves behind to allow new emotions to surface. However, when the poet represses emotion in his work (like anger, Blank suggests) other feelings get fatally stuck. Thus the poem 'Michael' presents a father impotent to address his loss and grief (of his land and Luke) and paralysed within a 'catatonic denial' disguised 'as acceptance'.[36] For Susan Wolfson, this acceptance leads the poet to 'lodge perishable visions in shrines' (like Michael's unfinished sheep-fold) 'that may preserve' or elegize them, but thwart their renewal or release. By contrast, Wolfson suggests, Dorothy refuses to bottle the emotional content of her visions, choosing instead to free them through restorative relationships with others.[37]

Feminist critics such as Wolfson and Anne Mellor suggest that Dorothy's writing is indifferent to the authoritative poetic 'I' that so oppresses Wordsworth speakers. These speakers not only ventriloquize the poet's insecure relationship to the 'role of creative artist as a political leader or religious saviour', Mellor contends, but also assist the poet in his efforts to steal 'from women their primary cultural authority as the experts in delicate, tender feelings and, by extension, moral purity and goodness'.[38] Gayatri Chakravorty Spivak similarly remarks that Wordsworth exploits women as blank slates upon which he can project and transcribe the troubles of his ego. Echoing Jacobus, she reads his coded descriptions of 'illegitimate paternity' in *The Prelude* as a technique wherein he can 're-establish himself sexually in order to declare his imagination restored'.[39]

For John Powell Ward, however, 'the power in Wordsworth's poetry lies not merely in cultural authority claimed over' questions of gender and the imagination, 'but in precisely the tension between such claims and the poet's clear vulnerability toward women and the feminine', one that influenced his work as much as his relationships with women.[40] 'Real' women, like Dorothy, Mary or Felicia Hemans, together with his more ethereal characters, for example, Lucy or the solitary reaper, tend to haunt Wordsworth's poems, as if the narrator continually fears their departure. By contrast, his abandoned women, Margaret, Martha Ray, Goody Blake, the forsaken Indian woman and the emigrant mother, seem to fill the poems, their suffering vividly and sympathetically evoked. Wordsworth uses this suffering in order to move himself and the reader closer to an understanding of the world to which he has no access without feminine presence. The girl he encounters by the gibbet mast in *The Prelude* (P, XI.306), for example, clarifies his vision by turning an otherwise dreary scene into a spot of time that serves to challenge and so develop his identity as a poet. She enables him in a similar way to his closest friend, Dorothy, who pervades so many of his poems – 'An Evening Walk', 'To A Butterfly', 'To My Sister', 'The Sparrow's Nest', 'Among All Lovely Things', 'Home at Grasmere', 'Tintern Abbey', the Lucy poems – that his canon is unthinkable without her.

Wordsworth's relationship to Dorothy is variously read as exploitative, sexualized and domestic, but Alan Grob perhaps comes closest to capturing the relationship between the brother and sister by figuring it through their shared love for and loyalty to one another.[41] Certainly the intimacy between Wordsworth and Dorothy, so central to feminist critiques of the poet, is impassioned: one only has to read Dorothy's account of lying silently down with her brother in the grave-like trench at John's Grove (a journal entry that closes with the words 'We went to bed immediately'); or her emotive account of wearing Mary's wedding ring the night before her brother's marriage. Yet Wordsworth is similarly impassioned about Coleridge and Crabb Robinson, as well as Mary, figures who steadied him, physically and emotionally, especially, psychoanalytic critics assert, in the absence of his mother.

It is in fact quite difficult to read Wordsworth as a Romantic patriarch once we acknowledge that his first published poem is a tribute to Helen Maria Williams, that his strongest representations of the poetic voice are spoken by women, and that nearly all of his most intimate friends, from Dorothy to Isabella Fenwick, are women. His planned anthology of women's writing – 'An Account of the Deceased Poetesses of Great Britain with an Estimation of Their Works' is also often overlooked. 'Neither Dr Johnson, nor Dr Anderson, nor Chalmers, nor the Editor I believe of any other Corpus of English Poetry', he wrote, 'takes the least notice of female Writers – this, to say nothing harsher, is very ungallant.'[42] As Marlon Ross argues, it is the women writers of the period who scripted the romantic ideologies and narratives with which poets like Wordsworth ended up working.[43]

Feminist readings are also concerned with Wordsworth's representation of gender, one that they argue is politically subversive, and able to dismantle normative assumptions about what it means to be a man or a woman. Adela Pinch, for example, suggests that Wordsworth's poetry strives to understand the gendered bodily and emotional effects of reading. She reads the Lucy poem, 'Strange Fits of Passion', as a text that genders the way metre excites and regulates emotion as it invites readers to think about Lucy's mysterious identity and why she haunts a poem about a narrator having a 'strange fit'. For Pinch, the most 'wayward and difficult to know' feelings – bodily, sexual and emotional – are 'poetically productive' for Wordsworth, even as his narrator's cry, '"O Mercy!"', in the penultimate line of the poem, recalls his declaration that poetry leaves us 'utterly at the mercy' of 'those arbitrary connections of feelings and ideas with particular words' (*PW*, I.145, 152).[44]

Elizabeth Fay also suggests Wordsworth's poetry is dependent on the female, but suggests that Wordsworth the poet (as opposed to Wordsworth the man) is a performance of 'two enacting selves: William and Dorothy Wordsworth combined'.[45] Reading the poet's work as inextricable from his love for Dorothy, Fay argues that Wordsworth relies on the poetic presence of his sister to reinstall love into those gaps left by Lucy's death, Margaret's suffering, the solitary reaper's perplexing lyric and so on. Rachel DuPlessis even suggests that Wordsworth's 'incomplete understanding' of the reaper is a self-conscious admission to the fear of personal inadequacy: the poet worries that, like the female subjects of his poems, he will not be understood either. The enunciation 'Will no one tell me what she sings' thus destabilizes readings of Wordsworth as poet and reaper as muse (Wordsworth passively listens to her inspired song) in order to reproduce, and then deconstruct, the social relations of gender and nation through which the reader must then negotiate the poem.[46]

Historicism and prosody

While DuPlessis is concerned to gender the relationship between poet and muse in 'The Solitary Reaper', her account also historicizes the poem by noting its debt to Gaelic culture. While early reviewers of Wordsworth's poetry often gestured towards its historical allusions, modern literary criticism has become dependent on history as a route into all aspects of the poet's life and work. Political history initially granted critics like E. P. Thompson and John Williams a way of affirming Wordsworth's democratic allegiance, one with which he may have become disenchanted, Thompson argues, but on which he did not default.[47] Nicholas Roe's sharp account of Wordsworth's early dissenting politics also revitalized depoliticized accounts of the poet, providing a bridge between anecdotal biography and an ideologically driven 'new' historicism.[48]

In contrast to the work of Thompson, Williams and Roe, however, 'new' historicism is typically suspicious of reading texts through 'past historical context', a technique that for Jerome McGann is 'fruitless and arid' because of its unwillingness to make explicit 'the dialectical relation of the analyzed "texts" to present interests and concerns'. He insists that only self-conscious patterns of reading 'return poetry to a human form', rooting it in a sense of history measured by immediate social concerns (for McGann, writing in the 1980s, these concerns included class, race, gender and sexuality).[49] As a result, new historicists trace modern politics back into Wordsworth's poetry, which they then find politically lacking (McGann) or ideologically conservative (James Chandler).[50] Marjorie Levinson similarly charges the poet with advocating 'undetermined and apolitical' values as a way to 'escape' from culture; while Alan Liu reads Wordsworth's key themes – affection, love, nature, the self, imagination, time – as strategies for avoiding 'real' social problems.[51] Unlike historicism, then, new historicism shares with deconstruction an interest in what is absent or displaced from the text, and asks that we read 'art' as ideological false consciousness.[52]

For some critics, however, new historicism can seem excessively combative. Grob, for example, argues that the new historicist is intent on assigning 'blame' to a text or author for politically or aesthetically failing the modern reader.[53] Critics of new historicism also suggest that it overlooks the pleasures of the text in order to highlight various political agendas. Levinson's analysis of 'Tintern Abbey', for example, reads the poem, not aesthetically, but as a 'great escape' from reality, negating both the town of Tintern and the abbey itself, while ignoring the vagrants and coal-barges that reside in its grounds. For Levinson, this renders the poem's 'pastoral prospect' a 'fragile affair' that is 'artfully assembled by acts of exclusion'. Wordsworth's famous 'still, sad music of humanity' serves only to drown 'out the noise produced by actual people in actual distress', she argues.[54]

Other new historicists agree with Levinson. Liu proposes that 'Tintern Abbey' is about the 'displaced stance' Wordsworth 'took toward political and social history when, in the aftermath of the French Revolution, he learned to digress into his own mind'. John Barrell too reads Wordsworth's last-minute turn to Dorothy as a strategy for demoting her intellectually from an independent reader of the world into a mere sisterly companion; while Judith Page suggests that, while Wordsworth recognizes himself in Dorothy, he nonetheless masculinizes his 'sister's lost narrative'.[55]

Critics like Grob, however, resist a criticism intent on condemning a poet for what he has not written, suggesting that Wordsworth's turn to Dorothy at the end of 'Tintern Abbey' constitutes the very radicalism new historicists bemoan is lacking from his work. His 'dear, dear Sister' is invoked as his moral and spiritual equal to forward a politics of egalitarianism and affection that new historicism's prosecutorial tactics ignore, as they do the poem's larger social programme, one that seeks to address and remedy the conditions in which the very people Levinson accuses Wordsworth of displacing live. Thomas McFarland too suggests that Levinson's reading represents 'a congeries' of modern critics more intent on establishing career paths by marketing new approaches to literature than on attending to Wordsworth's poetry.[56] For McFarland, new historicism's focus on what Wordsworth did not write at the expense of what he did evinces a lack of 'decorum' for the subject matter with which the discipline is concerned.

The formalist critic Simon Jarvis echoes this anxiety, accusing new historicism of 'damagingly disconnecting literary theory from philosophy'.[57] Jarvis seeks to repair this damage by reminding readers that Wordsworth chose to predominantly write poetry, not socio-political prose, a form or mode of thinking that is attentive to words, sounds, emotions and how they register in both the mind and the body. Rejecting a computational metric, Jarvis claims that Wordsworth's definition of prosody involves discernment and reflection, a method comprised of a series of thought processes that 'emerge in the course of inquiry'.[58] Echoing McFarland's call for a 'decorous' criticism, Jarvis urges us to ask those interpretive questions 'which concern fidelity to experience', reading poetry in a manner that feels emotionally and intellectually plausible for an individual reading in a specific time and place. Wordsworth, Jarvis argues, was committed to a poetry that looked 'steadily at its subject', his works 'acts of attention' that allow the reader to imaginatively occupy and affirm the poem by living in and experiencing it.[59]

This intense modern focus on what Wordsworth calls the 'music of the poem' is methodologically labelled the 'new prosody', and draws together critics who, like Jarvis, employ a newly politicized and cultural form of prosodic analysis to engage with poetic language. Critics such as Wolfson have always encouraged readers to think about how they enunciate the sounds of words as they read, inviting them to tune in to what T. S. Eliot called the 'auditory imagination' in which we consciously and unconsciously hear and feel 'syllable and rhythm'.[60] She argues that for Wordsworth, words signify through their capacity to 'imprint' observations and memories as sounds, his poems textual auditoriums in which the poet can amplify the past aurally. Wolfson refers to the ice-skating scene in *The Prelude*, for example, where the 'hiss' of the skates on 'polished ice' (I.461) transforms the lake into a 'sounding board' of ricocheting 's's.

The new prosody, then, like new historicism, asks the reader to reflect on old ideas (rhythm, metre, sound) in innovative ways (through philosophy, politics, history). Even Levinson has turned to debates about prosody in her recent work on Spinoza's influence on Wordsworth.[61] Spinoza, Levinson points out, also gives us access to another recently rehabilitated field, that of religion, once regarded as indiscriminately conservative and oppressive by a largely secular literary criticism that now appears willing to acknowledge its enabling impact on Wordsworth. While critics like Stephen Prickett have historicized this impact by detailing the various religious traditions available to Wordsworth, Jonathan Roberts suggests that the poet's anti-clerical and spiritualized vision is compatible not only with contemporary theology, but also with modern religious experience.[62]

Aesthetics and ethics

Renewed interest in Wordsworth's relationship with religion is partly a historical one, then, but it also marks a return to metaphysical, philosophical and ethical concerns newly configured in a politicized and theorized form. Ethical criticism, for example, asks whether or not it is appropriate either to assess literature in terms of morals and values, or to judge to what extent it might improve and cultivate the individual. For ethical critics, Wordsworth's poetry forges an aesthetic and linguistic way of encouraging the reader to reflect on his or her being, but does so through focusing on ways of relating, to one's friends, community, environment and God. As Adam Potkay argues, Wordsworth's poetry presents a 'lyric apprehension of the life of things, a life that human beings, with their passions and actions and words, share almost as equals with other thinking things and indeed with all things'. For Potkay, the historicist obsession with 'things' as material objects has distracted critical attention away from Wordsworth's attempt to '(re)insert us into a less reified world, one in which human and nonhuman activities are viewed as interanimate with objects, made and unmade'.[63]

Paul Fry agrees, arguing that Wordsworth's poetry 'has a far more radical, pressing and original motive' than history or politics in its ontic concern for the 'unsemantic self-identity of things'. Invested as he is in the commonality of all things throughout his writing, Wordsworth consistently calls for a poetry that 'helps the imagination respond to the world with fitting intensity' while also provoking fellow-feeling for all modes of being.[64] Wordsworth's proclamation in *The Excursion*: 'Happy is He who lives to understand! / Not human Nature only, but explores / All Natures' (IV.335–7) speaks to Potkay and Fry's attention to the relationship between things in the world, but also resonates with Donna Haraway's work on 'companion species'. Haraway argues that the way humans interact, co-habit and co-evolve with other companionable organic beings (from grains of rice and bees, to tulips and dogs) produces the grounds from which 'the worlds we might yet live in' emerge.[65]

Certainly the unusual domestic household in which Wordsworth lived with Mary, Dorothy, Coleridge and various other friends, relatives and his dogs 'Music' and 'Fidelity' developed precisely from the poet's ability to rethink interaction with people and nature as inclusive and interdependent. Hugh Sykes Davies suggests that such a household would have necessarily developed a distinctive idiolectic language, in which words take on shared, intimate and evolving meanings that at once spark conversation and deepen connections between people.[66] Rhian Williams and I suggest that Wordsworth's poetry responds particularly well to communal and habitual reading practices, and use the phrase 'reciprocal scansion' to describe a shared practice of prosodic interpretation that takes into account the subjective, cultural and regional ways different readers hear and see his words. Reciprocal scansion not only names a backward–forward movement of reading and rereading Wordsworth's verse, but also understands his poems as sites of communication and recognition between readers.[67]

For Wayne Booth, ethical criticism is also dependent on shared reading or what he calls 'coduction', the process of agreeing on the ethical value of a text through conversation with others.[68] These 'others', argue critics such as Haraway and Jonathan Bate, should also include the natural world, that which we need to learn to live with, rather than use as a surrogate for theory or history. For Bate, Wordsworth's very project consists of enabling 'his readers better to enjoy or endure life' by 'teaching them to look at and dwell in the natural world'. In doing so, readers are freed to develop an ecological 'attitude of mind' that has the potential to engender 'an effective set of environmental policies'.[69] Centralizing geography rather than history, then, green critics focus our attention on Wordsworth's 'ecopoetics'. As Toby Benis shows, for example, Wordsworth's ecological support of pedestrian travel is both political (he encourages his readers to walk everywhere) and also aesthetic (his narrators often see the world from the perspective of a pedestrian).[70]

Like Bate, Nicholas Roe also contends that a critical focus on Wordsworth's politics of nature opens up discussion of urgent modern environmental issues, but returns to the idea of Wordsworth as a radical humanist whose work is consistently suggestive of his 'kindly emphasis on human community', benevolence and love.[71] For David Bromwich, Wordsworth's investment in the 'humanizing power of sympathy' is revealed in his focus on the 'ethical act' of 'attention' to others, his poems issuing 'from a feeling by one person about someone or something human'. This feeling, however, is not reciprocal for Bromwich, Wordsworth being concerned only with 'the way things feel to a seeing self': this is why he is interested primarily 'in people who continue to be themselves, who insist on themselves, weirdly or helplessly, whatever the cost to utility and convention'.[72]

Modern criticism, then, remains captivated by the question of feeling that Wordsworth began his poetic career exploring, and continues to debate its habitual, accidental but compelling quality through theories of affect, histories of sensibility and revisionary approaches to humanism.[73] For critics like Hartman, Ferguson, Bromwich and Bate, feeling remains as much an ethical and moral arena of thought as an aesthetic one and so returns us to those questions that once preoccupied Mill, Ruskin and Arnold. New work on prosody and 'rhythm-analysis' pushes these interests further by exploring the sensations metre elicits in the mind and in the body, as do studies of affect and religion that ask to what extent Wordsworth's 'natural feeling' leads to moral belief in and responsibility to one's community and surroundings.[74] Such work continues to highlight the timely, if always peculiar, nature of Wordsworth's poetry.

Notes

Preface

1 Samuel Taylor Coleridge, letter to Richard Sharp, 15 January 1804.
2 John Stuart Mill, *Autobiography* (1873), in John M. Robson and Jack Stillinger, eds., *Autobiography and Literary Essays* (Toronto: University of Toronto Press, 1981), pp.1–290 (p.153).
3 Samuel Taylor Coleridge, *Biographia Literaria, or, Biographical Sketches of my Literary Life and Opinions*, 2 vols, in James Engell and W. Jackson Bate, eds., *The Collected Works of Samuel Taylor Coleridge*, 16 vols. (Princeton: Princeton University Press, 1983), VII, ii, p.7.
4 David Bromwich, *Disowned by Memory: Wordsworth's Poetry of the 1790s* (Chicago: University of Chicago Press, 1998), p.42 fn.12; William Wordsworth, letter to Margaret Beaumont, 21 May 1807.

Chapter 1

1 Juliet Barker, *William Wordsworth: A Life in Letters* (London: Penguin, 2007), p.7.
2 William Wordsworth, letter to William Mathews, 3 August 1791.
3 William Wordsworth, letter to Dorothy Wordsworth, 6/16 September 1790.
4 Dorothy Wordsworth, letter to Jane Pollard, 8 May 1792.
5 Dorothy Wordsworth, letter to Jane Pollard, 16 February 1793.
6 Richard Wordsworth, letter to William Wordsworth, 23 May 1794.
7 Dorothy Wordsworth, letter to Mary Hutchinson, 14 August 1797.
8 Dorothy Wordsworth, letter to Mary Hutchinson, n.d. June 1797; Samuel Taylor Coleridge, letters to Joseph Cottle, 3 July 1797 and 7 March 1798.
9 H. D. Rawnsley, *Reminiscences of Wordsworth among the Peasantry of Westmoreland* (London: Dillon's, 1968), pp.32, 13.
10 Daniel Lysons, letter to William Cavendish-Bentinck, 11 August 1797, in Patrick J. Keane, *Coleridge's Submerged Politics: The Ancient Mariner and Robinson Crusoe* (Columbia: University of Missouri Press, 1994), p.300.
11 Samuel Taylor Coleridge, letter to William Wordsworth, 10 September 1799.

12 William and Dorothy Wordsworth, letter to Samuel Taylor Coleridge, 24/27 December 1799.

13 William Wordsworth, letter to George Beaumont, 23 February 1805.

14 Dorothy Wordsworth, letter to Jane Marshall, 29 September 1802.

15 Dorothy Wordsworth, 4 October 1802, in Pamela Woof, ed., *The Grasmere and Alfoxden Journals* (Oxford: Oxford University Press, 2002), p.126.

16 Samuel Taylor Coleridge, letter to Richard Sharp, 15 January 1804.

17 Samuel Taylor Coleridge, letter to Mrs John Thelwall, 22 November 1803.

18 In Kathleen Coburn, ed., *The Notebooks of Samuel Taylor Coleridge*, 5 vols. (Princeton: Princeton University Press, 1957–2002), I, notes 1782, 1801.

19 William Wordsworth, letter to Thomas De Quincey, 6 March 1804; and letter to George Beaumont, 3 June 1805.

20 William Wordsworth, letter to Richard Wordsworth, 11 February 1805.

21 William Wordsworth, letter to James Losh, 16 March 1805.

22 William Wordsworth, letter to Mary Wordsworth, 22 July 1810; Mary Wordsworth, letter to William Wordsworth, 23 May 1812.

23 Dorothy Wordsworth, letters to Jane Pollard, 26 June 1791; and 16 February 1793.

24 Sara Hutchinson, letter to Mary Monkhouse, 27 October 1811, in Juliet Barker, *Wordsworth: A Life* (London: Viking, 2000), p.419.

25 Dorothy Wordsworth, letter to William Wordsworth, 31 March 1808.

26 William Wordsworth, letter to Margaret Beaumont, 21 May 1807.

27 *Monthly Literary Recreations*, 3 (July 1808), 65–6; *Critical Review*, 11 (August 1807), 399–403; *Satirist*, 1 (November 1807), 188–91; *Cabinet*, 3 (April 1808), 249–52; *Eclectic Review*, 4 (January 1808), 35–43; *The Examiner*, 28 August 1808; all in Stephen Gill, *William Wordsworth: A Life* (Oxford: Oxford University Press, 1989), pp.266–7.

28 Dorothy Wordsworth, letters to Catherine Clarkson, 8 December 1808, 12 April 1810 and 12 November 1810.

29 Coburn, ed., *Notebooks of Coleridge*, III, notes 3991, 3997.

30 Catherine Clarkson, letter to Henry Crabb Robinson, 29 March 1813.

31 William Wordsworth, letter to Catherine Clarkson, n.d. January 1815.

32 *Edinburgh Review*, 25 (October 1815), 353–63.

33 *European Magazine*, 77 (June 1820), 523.

34 *Edinburgh Review*, 37 (November 1822), 449.

35 Coburn, ed., *Notebooks of Coleridge*, V, notes 5902, 5904.

36 Dorothy Wordsworth, letter to Mary Lamb, 9 January 1830.

37 William Wordsworth, letter to Samuel Rogers, 15 August 1825.

38 William Wordsworth, letter to Dora and Mary Wordsworth, 21 June 1827.

39 Jared Curtis, ed., *The Fenwick Notes of William Wordsworth* (London: Bristol Classical Press, 1993).

40 Mary Wordsworth, letter to Isabella Fenwick, 13 May 1846.

Chapter 2

1 For 'Great God! I'd rather be / A Pagan', see lines 9–10 of Wordsworth's sonnet, 'The World Is Too Much with Us' (composed 1802–4; published 1807).

2 Joseph Priestley, *An Examination of Dr Reid's Inquiry into the Human Mind etc.* (London: J. Johnson, 1774), xix.

3 Humphry Davy, 'A Discourse Introductory to a Course of Lectures on Chemistry', in John Davy, ed., *The Collected Works of Sir Humphry Davy*, 9 vols. (London: Smith, Elder and Co., 1839), II, pp.307–26.

4 Joseph Priestley, 'The Importance and Extent of Free Inquiry in Matters of Religion', in J. T. Rutt, ed., *The Theological and Miscellaneous Works, & c., of Joseph Priestley*, 25 vols. (London, 1818), XVIII, p.544.

5 Jürgen Habermas, *The Structural Transformation of the Public Sphere: An Inquiry into a Category of Bourgeois Society*, trans. Thomas Burger and Frederick Lawrence (Cambridge: Polity Press, 1989), pp.25–6.

6 Edmund Burke, *A Philosophical Enquiry into the Sublime and Beautiful* (London: Penguin, 2004), p.101.

7 Richard Price, *Discourse on the Love of our Country* (London: George Stafford, 1789), p.40.

8 Edmund Burke, *Reflections on the Revolution in France, and on the Proceedings in Certain Societies in London Relative to that Event* (Harmondsworth: Penguin, 1968), pp.126, 339.

9 Richard Wordsworth, letter to William Wordsworth, 23 May 1794.

10 See John Barrell, *Imagining the King's Death: Figurative Treason, Fantasies of Regicide, 1793–1796* (Oxford: Oxford University Press, 2000).

11 Dorothy Wordsworth, letter to Catherine Clarkson, 9 October 1803.

12 William Wordsworth, letter to Charles James Fox, 14 January 1801.

13 Quoted in Michael Turner, *Enclosures in Britain, 1750–1830* (London: Macmillan, 1984), p.23.

14 See Alan Bewell, *Wordsworth and the Enlightenment: Nature, Man, and Society in the Experimental Poetry* (New Haven: Yale University Press, 1989).

15 James Chandler, *Wordsworth's Second Nature: A Study of the Poetry and Politics* (Chicago: University of Chicago Press, 1984).

16 John Wesley, 'Sermon 98: On Visiting the Sick' [1786], in Albert C. Outler, ed., *The Works of John Wesley: Sermons III: 71–114*, 26 vols. (Nashville: Abingdon Press, 1986), III, pp.384–97 (p.396).

17 Hannah More, *Strictures on the Modern System of Education* (London: Cadell and Davies, 1802), II, p.30.

18 See Samuel Taylor Coleridge, *Table Talk*, ed. Carl Woodring, 2 vols. (Princeton: Princeton University Press, 1990), II, p.190 (1 September 1832).

19 John Keats, letter to J. H. Reynolds, 3 May 1818, in Robert Gittings, ed., *Letters of John Keats* (Oxford: Oxford University Press, 1970), pp.90–7.

20 Geoffrey Hartman, *The Unremarkable Wordsworth* (London: Methuen, 1987), p.153.
21 William Wordsworth, letter to Henry Alford, 20 February 1840; Samuel Taylor Coleridge, letter to John Thelwall, 13 May 1796.
22 John Henry Newman, *Apologia Pro Vita Sua* (London: Penguin, 1994), p.100.
23 John Keble, *Lectures on Poetry, 1832–1841*, trans. E. K. Francis (Oxford: Clarendon Press, 1912).
24 John Keble, 'Life of Sir Walter Scott', *British Critic* (1838), in Keble, *Occasional Papers and Reviews* (Oxford and London: James Parker and Co., 1877), pp.1–80.

Chapter 3

1 Marilyn Butler, *Romantics, Rebels and Reactionaries: English Literature and Its Background 1760–1830* (Oxford: Oxford University Press, 1981), p.58.
2 William Hazlitt, *The Spirit of the Age*, in *The Complete Works of William Hazlitt*, ed. P. P. Howe, 21 vols. (New York: AMS Press, 1967), XI, p.132.
3 William Wordsworth, letter to John Wilson, 7 June 1802.
4 Dorothy Wordsworth, letter to Margaret Beaumont, 29 November 1805.
5 Walter Pater, 'Wordsworth' (1874), in *Appreciations* (London: Macmillan, 1910), pp.39–64 (p.58).
6 P. B. Shelley, 'A Defense of Poetry', in Donald H. Reiman, ed., *Shelley's Poetry and Prose* (New York: Norton, 1977), pp.480–508 (p.486).
7 Dorothy Wordsworth, 15 June 1802, in Woof, ed., *Journals*, p.109.
8 Rawnsley, *Reminiscences*, p.18.
9 William Wordsworth, letter to Catherine Godwin, n.d., spring 1829.
10 John Milton, 'The Verse', in *Paradise Lost* (New York: Norton, 1993), p.6.
11 Simon Jarvis, *Wordsworth's Philosophic Song* (Cambridge: Cambridge University Press, 2007), p.8.
12 Coleridge, *Biographia*, VII, ii, p.79; William Wordsworth, letter to John Thelwall, n.d. January 1804.
13 Brennan O'Donnell, *The Passion of Metre: A Study of Wordsworth's Metrical Art* (Ohio: Kent State University Press, 1995), pp.180–8.
14 Curtis, ed., *Fenwick Notes*, p.19.
15 *The Gentleman's Magazine*, 14 (1840), 624; and 16 (1841), 510.
16 *Edinburgh Review*, 11 (1807), 230.
17 William Wordsworth, letter to W. S. Landor, 20 April 1822.
18 Samuel Taylor Coleridge, letter to Joseph Cottle, 7 March 1815.
19 William Wordsworth, letter to Alexander Dyce, 22 April 1833.
20 *The Athenaeum* (30 January 1836), p.88.
21 Curtis, ed., *Fenwick Notes*, p.61.
22 William Wordsworth, letter to W. S. Landor, 21 January 1824.

23 Dorothy Wordsworth, letter to John Marshall, 15/17 March 1805.

24 John Wordsworth, letter to Mary Hutchinson, 12 September 1802.

25 William Wordsworth, letter to George Beaumont, 11 February 1805.

Chapter 4

1 Dorothy Wordsworth, letter to Sara Hutchinson, 14 June 1802.

2 John Keats, letter to J. H. Reynolds, 3 May 1818, in Gittings, ed., *Letters*, pp.90–7.

3 Gilbert White, *The Natural History of Selborne* (London: Penguin, 1987).

4 Mary Jacobus, *Tradition and Experiment in Wordsworth's Lyrical Ballads (1798)* (Oxford: Clarendon Press, 1976), p.135; Alan Liu, *Wordsworth: The Sense of History* (Stanford: Stanford University Press, 1989), see chapter 3; Stephen Gill, ed., *The Salisbury Plain Poems of William Wordsworth* (Ithaca: Cornell University Press, 1975).

5 Thomas De Quincey, 'On Wordsworth's Poetry', *Tait's Edinburgh Magazine* (1845), repr. in *De Quincey as Critic*, ed. John E. Jordan (London: Routledge and Kegan Paul, 1973), pp.407–9.

6 Adela Pinch, 'Female Chatter: Meter, Masochism, and the *Lyrical Ballads*', *English Literary History*, 55.4 (1988), 835–52 (846).

7 Samuel Taylor Coleridge, letter to Tom Poole, 6 April 1799; and William Wordsworth, letter to Samuel Taylor Coleridge, 14/21 December 1798.

8 Samuel Butler, *Essays on Art, Life and Science* (London, 1904).

9 Thomas De Quincey, *Recollections of the Lakes and the Lake Poets* (Harmondsworth: Penguin, 1970), pp.159–60.

10 William Wordsworth, letter to Charles James Fox, 14 January 1801.

11 Review of *Poems, in Two Volumes* (1807), in *The Critical Review, or Annals of Literature*, XI (1807), 403.

12 Quotations from 'To the Cuckoo', 4; 'The Sparrow's Nest', 1; 'To a Sky-Lark', 4; 'The Green Linnet', 21; 'To the Small Celandine', 56; all poems composed in 1802.

13 Thomas Wilkinson, *Tours to the British Mountains with the Descriptive Poems of Lowther, and Emont Vale* (London, 1824), in Jared R. Curtis, ed., *William Wordsworth: Poems in Two Volumes* (Ithaca, NY: Cornell University Press, 1983), p.415.

14 In Christopher Wordsworth, *Memoirs of William Wordsworth*, 2 vols. (Boston, MA: Ticknor, Reed and Fields, 1851), II, p.313.

15 Curtis, ed., *Fenwick Notes*, p.33.

16 William Wordsworth, letter to Robert Southey, n.d. June 1816; and to Coleridge, 19 April 1808.

17 Coleridge, *Biographia*, VII, i, p.305.

18 Paul de Man, 'Intentional Structure of the Romantic Image', in M. H. Abrams, ed., *Wordsworth: A Collection of Critical Essays* (Englewood Cliffs: Prentice Hall, 1972), pp.133–44.

19 See Hazlitt, *The Spirit of the Age*, in Howe, ed., *Complete Works*, VII, p.91.

Chapter 5

1 Hartman, *Unremarkable Wordsworth*, p.17.
2 Mary Moorman, *William Wordsworth: A Biography*, 2 vols. (London: Oxford University Press, 1968); Gill, *William Wordsworth: A Life*; Barker, *Wordsworth* and *Letters*; Keith Hanley, *Wordsworth: A Poet's History* (Basingstoke: Palgrave, 2001); Duncan Wu, *Wordsworth: An Inner Life* (Oxford: Blackwell, 2002); Pamela Woof, *Dorothy Wordsworth: Writer* (Grasmere: Wordsworth Trust, 1988); Frances Wilson, *The Ballad of Dorothy Wordsworth* (London: Faber and Faber, 2008); Lucy Newlyn, *Reading, Writing, and Romanticism: The Anxiety of Reception* (Oxford: Oxford University Press, 2000).
3 Bernard Groom, *The Unity of Wordsworth's Poetry* (London: Macmillan, 1966); Frances Ferguson, *Wordsworth: Language as Counter-Spirit* (New Haven: Yale University Press, 1977).
4 Mill, *Autobiography*, pp.151–3.
5 Felicia Hemans, 'Preface' to *Scenes and Hymns of Life* (Edinburgh: William Blackwood; London: T. Cadell, 1834); for detail on the Victorians' devotion to Wordsworth, see Stephen Gill, *Wordsworth and the Victorians* (Oxford: Clarendon Press, 1998).
6 Henry N. Hudson, *Studies in Wordsworth* (Boston, MA: Little, Brown and Co., 1884), in Gill, *Wordsworth and the Victorians*, p.4.
7 William Wordsworth, letter to George Beaumont, n.d., February 1808.
8 William Blake, 1826 annotation to Wordsworth's *Poems* (1815), in David V. Erdman, ed., *The Poetry and Prose of William Blake* (New York: Doubleday, 1965), p.654; Francis Jeffrey, review of *Poems in Two Volumes* (1807), in the *Edinburgh Review*, 11 (October, 1807), in Graham McMaster, ed., *William Wordsworth* (Harmondsworth: Penguin, 1972), pp.92–6; William Hazlitt, 'Mr Wordsworth', in Geoffrey Keynes, ed., *Selected Essays* (London: Nonesuch Press, 1934), pp.739–51 (p.751).
9 Matthew Arnold, *Poems of Wordsworth* (London: Macmillan, 1879), xxiv.
10 John Keble, *Memoir of the Rev. John Keble* (Oxford and London: James Parker, 1869), p.249.
11 A. C. Swinburne, 'Wordsworth and Byron', *Miscellanies* (London: Chatto and Windus, 1886), pp.63–156 (pp.114, 117).
12 John Ruskin, letter to Walter Lucas Brown, 20 December 1843, in E. T. Cook and Alexander Wedderburn, *The Works of John Ruskin*, 39 vols. (London: George Allen, 1903–12), IV, pp.390–3 (p.392).
13 Dora Greenwell, letter to William Knight, 5 April 1866, in William Dorling, *Memoirs of Dora Greenwell* (London: James Clarke and Co., 1885), p.102; Gerard Manley Hopkins, letter to R. W. Dixon, 23 October 1886, in Claude Colleer Abbott, ed., *The Correspondence of Gerard Manley Hopkins and Richard Watson Dixon* (London: Oxford University Press, 1935), pp.145–9.
14 Pater, 'Wordsworth', p.50.

15 A. C. Bradley, 'Wordsworth' (1909), in M. H. Abrams, ed. *Wordsworth: A Collection of Critical Essays* (Englewood Cliffs: Prentice Hall, 1972), pp.13–21 (pp.13, 16).

16 G. M. Harper, *Wordsworth's French Daughter: The Story of Her Birth, with the Certificates of Her Baptism and Marriage* (Princeton: Princeton University Press, 1921); and Emile Legouis, *William Wordsworth and Annette Vallon* (London: J. M. Dent, 1922).

17 Herbert Read, *Wordsworth* (London: Cape, 1930); F. W. Bateson, *Wordsworth: A Reinterpretation* (London: Longman, 1954).

18 W. K. Wimsatt and Monroe Beardsley, 'The Affective Fallacy', *The Sewanee Review*, 57.1 (1949), 3–27.

19 T. S. Eliot, 'Wordsworth and Coleridge', *The Use of Poetry and the Use of Criticism* (London: Faber and Faber, 1964), pp.67–85; F. R. Leavis, *Revaluation: Tradition and Development in English Poetry* (London: Penguin, 1936), pp.146, 15.

20 John Dewey, *Art as Experience* (London: Allen and Unwin, 1934).

21 See, for example, Ernest de Selincourt and Helen Darbishire, eds., *The Poetical Works of William Wordsworth* (Oxford: Clarendon Press, 1947); Enid Welsford, *Salisbury Plain: A Study of the Development of Wordsworth's Mind and Art* (Oxford: Blackwell, 1966).

22 Cleanth Brooks, *The Well Wrought Urn: Studies in the Structure of Poetry* (New York: Harcourt Brace, 1947); John Jones, *The Egotistical Sublime: A History of Wordsworth's Imagination* (London: Chatto and Windus, 1954).

23 M. H. Abrams, *The Mirror and the Lamp: Romantic Theory and the Critical Tradition* (Oxford: Oxford University Press, 1953), p.103.

24 M. H. Abrams, *Natural Supernaturalism: Tradition and Revolution in Romantic Literature* (New York: Norton, 1971), pp.27–37.

25 Geoffrey H. Hartman, *Scars of the Spirit: The Struggle against Inauthenticity* (New York: Palgrave, 2002), p.173.

26 On Hartman's 'psychoaesthetics', see *The Fate of Reading and Other Essays* (Chicago: Chicago University Press, 1975); on his idea of 'theopoesis', see ' "Was It for This?: Wordsworth and the Birth of the Gods', in Kenneth R. Johnston, ed., *Romantic Revolutions: Criticism and Theory* (Bloomington: University of Indiana Press, 1990), pp.8–25.

27 Geoffrey Hartman, *Wordsworth's Poetry 1787–1814* (New Haven: Yale University Press, 1964).

28 Geoffrey H. Hartman, *A Scholar's Tale: Intellectual Journey of a Displaced Child of Europe* (New York: Fordham University Press, 2007), pp.22, 160.

29 Hartman, *Unremarkable Wordsworth*, pp.16–17.

30 Harold Bloom, *The Anxiety of Influence: A Theory of Poetry* (New York: Oxford University Press, 1973); Paul de Man, 'Intentional Structure of the Romantic Image', in Harold Bloom, ed., *Romanticism and Consciousness* (New York: Norton, 1970), pp.65–77; Christopher Ricks, *The Force of Poetry* (Oxford: Clarendon Press, 1984); Jonathan Wordsworth, *The Music of Humanity: A Critical Study of Wordsworth's*

'*Ruined Cottage*' (London: Nelson, 1969); Kenneth R. Johnston, *Wordsworth and The Recluse* (New Haven: Yale University Press, 1984).

31 William A. Ulmer, *The Christian Wordsworth 1798–1805* (New York: State University of New York Press, 2001).

32 James A. W. Heffernan, 'The Presence of the Absent Mother in Wordsworth's *Prelude*', *Studies in Romanticism*, 27.2 (1988), 253–72; Diane Hoeveler Long, *Romantic Androgyny: The Woman Within* (University Park: Penn State University Press, 1990); Alan Richardson, 'Romanticism and the Colonization of the Feminine', in Anne K. Mellor, ed., *Romanticism and Feminism* (Bloomington: University of Indiana Press, 1988), pp.13–25; Mary Jacobus, *Romanticism, Writing, and Sexual Difference: Essays on The Prelude* (Oxford: Clarendon Press, 1989).

33 Rachel Crawford, 'The Structure of the Sororal in Wordsworth's "Nutting"', *Studies in Romanticism*, 31.2 (1992), 197–211; Charles Altieri, 'Wordsworth and the Options for Contemporary American Poetry', in Gene W. Ruoff, ed., *The Romantics and Us: Essays on Literature and Culture* (New Brunswick: Rutgers University Press, 1990), pp.184–212; David Perkins, *Wordsworth and the Poetry of Sincerity* (Cambridge, MA: Harvard University Press, 1964); Robert Burns Neveldine, 'Wordsworth's "Nutting" and the Violent End of Reading', *English Literary History*, 63.3 (1996), 657–80.

34 Jacobus, *Romanticism, Writing*, pp.238, 292.

35 Jean H. Hagstrum, *The Romantic Body: Love and Sexuality in Keats, Wordsworth, and Blake* (Knoxville: University of Tennessee Press, 1985).

36 G. Kim Blank, *Wordsworth and Feeling: The Poetry of an Adult Child* (London: Associated University Presses, 1995), p.31.

37 Susan J. Wolfson, 'Individual in Community: Dorothy Wordsworth in Conversation with William', in Anne K. Mellor, ed., *Romanticism and Feminism* (Bloomington: University of Indiana Press, 1988), pp.139–66.

38 Anne K. Mellor, 'A Criticism of Their Own: Romantic Women Literary Critics', in John Beer, ed., *Questioning Romanticism* (Baltimore: Johns Hopkins University Press, 1995), pp.29–48 (p.31); *Romanticism and Gender* (New York and London: Routledge, 1993), pp.23–4.

39 Gayari Chakravorty Spivak, 'Sex and History in *The Prelude* (1805): Books IX to XIII', in Richard Machin and Christopher Norris, eds., *Post-structuralist Readings of English Poetry* (Cambridge: Cambridge University Press, 1987), pp.193–226 (pp.193–5).

40 John Powell Ward, '"Will No One Tell Me What She Sings?": Women and Gender in the Poetry of William Wordsworth', *Studies in Romanticism*, 36.4 (1997), 611–33.

41 Alan Grob, 'William and Dorothy: A Case Study in the Hermeneutics of Disparagement', *English Literary History*, 65.1 (1998), 187–221.

42 William Wordsworth, letter to Dionysius Lardner, 12 January 1829.

43 Marlon B. Ross, *The Contours of Masculine Desire: Romanticism and the Rise of Women's Poetry* (Oxford: Oxford University Press, 1989).

44 Adela Pinch, *Strange Fits of Passion: Epistemologies of Emotion, Hume to Austen* (Stanford: Stanford University Press, 1996), pp.109–10.

45 Elizabeth A. Fay, *Becoming Wordsworthian: A Performative Aesthetics* (Amherst: University of Massachusetts Press, 1995), p.3.

46 Rachel Blau DuPlessis, 'Marble Paper: Toward a Feminist "History of Poetry"', *Modern Language Quarterly*, 65.1 (2004), 93–129 (109, 128).

47 E. P. Thompson, *The Romantics: England in a Revolutionary Age* (Woodbridge, Suffolk: Merlin Press, 1997); John Williams, *Wordsworth: Romantic Theory and Revolution Politics* (Manchester: Manchester University Press, 1989).

48 Nicholas Roe, *Wordsworth and Coleridge: The Radical Years* (Oxford: Clarendon Press, 1988).

49 Jerome J. McGann, *The Romantic Ideology: A Critical Investigation* (Chicago: University of Chicago Press, 1983), p.160.

50 Chandler, *Wordsworth's Second Nature*.

51 Marjorie Levinson, *Wordsworth's Great Period Poems: Four Essays* (Cambridge: Cambridge University Press, 1986), p.16; Liu, *Sense of History*, p.48.

52 See David Simpson, *Wordsworth's Historical Imagination: The Poetry of Displacement* (London: Methuen, 1987).

53 Grob, 'William and Dorothy', 187.

54 Levinson, *Four Essays*, p.45.

55 Liu, *Sense of History*, p.216; John Barrell, 'The Uses of Dorothy: "The Language of the Sense" in "Tintern Abbey"', *Poetry, Language, and Politics* (London: St Martin's Press, 1988), pp.137–67; Judith W. Page, *Wordsworth and the Cultivation of Women* (Berkeley and Los Angeles: University of California Press, 1994), pp.44–8.

56 Thomas McFarland, *William Wordsworth: Intensity and Achievement* (Oxford: Clarendon Press, 1992), pp.32–3.

57 Simon Jarvis, 'The Eucharistic Spud', review of Catherine Gallagher and Stephen Greenblatt, eds., *Practicing New Historicism* (Chicago: University of Chicago Press, 2000), in the *Times Literary Supplement* (13 October 2000), p.27.

58 Simon Jarvis, 'Prosody as Cognition', *Critical Quarterly*, 40.4 (1998), 3–15 (9, 12).

59 Jarvis, *Philosophic Song*, pp.32, 85, 223.

60 Susan Wolfson, 'Sounding Romantic: The Sound of Sound', *Romantic Circles Praxis Series*, April (2008), http://romantic.arhu.umd.edu/praxis/soundings/wolfson/wolfson.html; see T. S. Eliot, 'Matthew Arnold', *Use of Poetry*, pp.103–19 (p.118).

61 Marjorie Levinson, 'A Motion and a Spirit: Romancing Spinoza', *Studies in Romanticism*, 46.4 (2007), 367–408.

62 Stephen Prickett, *Romanticism and Religion: The Tradition of Coleridge and Wordsworth in the Victorian Church* (Cambridge: Cambridge University Press, 1976); Jonathan Roberts, *Blake. Wordsworth. Religion.* (London: Continuum, 2010).

63 Adam Potkay, 'Wordsworth and the Ethics of Things', *PMLA*, 123.2 (2008), 390–404 (400–1).

64 Paul H. Fry, *Wordsworth and the Poetry of What We Are* (New Haven: Yale University Press, 2008), pp.2–12.

65 Donna Haraway, *The Companion Species Manifesto: Dogs, People, and Significant Otherness* (Chicago: Prickly Paradigm Press, 2003), pp.3–4, 15.

66 Hugh Sykes Davies, *Wordsworth and the Worth of Words* (Cambridge: Cambridge University Press, 1986).

67 Emma Mason and Rhian Williams, 'Reciprocal Scansion in Wordsworth's "There Was a Boy"', *Literature Compass*, 6.2 (2009), 515–23.

68 Wayne C. Booth, *The Company We Keep: An Ethics of Fiction* (Berkeley: University of California Press, 1988).

69 Jonathan Bate, *Romantic Ecology: Wordsworth and the Environmental Tradition* (London: Routledge, 1991), pp.4, 83.

70 Toby R. Benis, *Romanticism on the Road: The Marginal Gains of Wordsworth's Homeless* (Basingstoke: Macmillan, 2000).

71 Nicholas Roe, *The Politics of Nature: William Wordsworth and Some Contemporaries* (Basingstoke: Palgrave, 2002), pp.9, 84.

72 Bromwich, *Disowned by Memory*, pp.40, 15, 108, 172–4.

73 See Emma Mason and Isobel Armstrong, eds., special issue:'Languages of Emotion', *Textual Practice*, 22.1 (2008); and Andy Mousley and Martin Halliwell, *Critical Humanisms: Humanist and Anti-humanist Debates* (Edinburgh: Edinburgh University Press, 2003).

74 Henri Lefebvre, *Rhythmanalysis: Space, Time and Everyday Life* (London: Continuum, 2004).

Guide to further reading

Wordsworth's poetry should always be the focal point of your reading, but the extensive criticism written on his work can enable or speak to your own reflections. To date, the only journal dedicated to Wordsworth and his associates is *The Wordsworth Circle*, but there are frequent articles on and about him in *Studies in Romanticism, European Romantic Review, Romanticism* and *The Charles Lamb Bulletin*. For an annual index of and commentary on new criticism on the poet, readers are advised to refer to the annual *The Year's Work in English Studies*. The following guide is indicative only, but the first titles listed in each grouping serve as introductions to the subject. Ten fields of criticism are outlined here: Textual issues; Biography; Poetics; Major poems; Philosophy and religion; Psychoanalysis and gender; Politics and historicism; Eco- and ethical criticism; Reception and influence; and Reference.

Textual issues: for information on available primary texts, see my note on 'Texts'; for the politics and psychology of Wordsworth's revisions, see Jerome McGann, *A Critique of Modern Textual Criticism* (Chicago: University of Chicago Press, 1983); William Galperin, *Revision and Authority in Wordsworth: The Interpretation of a Career* (Philadelphia: University of Pennsylvania Press, 1989); and Robert Brinkley and Keith Hanley, *Romantic Revisions* (Cambridge: Cambridge University Press, 1992). Further commentary can be found in Jack Stillinger, 'Textual Primitivism and the Editing of Wordsworth', *Studies in Romanticism*, 28:1 (1989), 3–28; and Kathryn Sutherland, 'Revised Relations? Material Text, Immaterial Text, and the Electronic Environment', *Text*, 11 (1998), 16–39. On *The Prelude*, which tends to dominate editorial debates, see Jonathan Wordsworth and Stephen Gill, '*The Two-Part Prelude* of 1798–99', *Journal of English and Germanic Philology*, 72:4 (1973), 503–25; Robin Jarvis, 'The Five-Book *Prelude*: A Reconsideration', *Journal of English and Germanic Philology*, 80:4 (1981), 528–51; and Herbert Lindenberger, Norman Fruman, Robert J. Barth and Jeffrey Baker, 'Waiting for the Palfreys: The Great *Prelude* Debate', *The Wordsworth Circle*, 17:1 (1986). On the 'Ruined Cottage' manuscripts, see John Alban Finch, ' "The Ruined Cottage" Restored: Three Stages of Composition', in Jonathan

121

Wordsworth and Beth Darlington, eds., *Bicentenary Wordsworth Studies in Memory of John Alban Finch* (Ithaca, NY: Cornell University Press, 1970), pp.29–49. Stephen Gill, 'Wordsworth's Poems: The Question of Text', *Review of English Studies*, 34.134 (1983), 172–90; Stephen Parrish, 'The Editor as Archaeologist', *Kentucky Review*, 4 (1983), 3–14; Duncan Wu, 'Editing Intentions', *Essays in Criticism*, 41:1 (1991), 1–10; and Andrew Bennett, *Wordsworth Writing* (Cambridge: Cambridge University Press, 2007) are also helpful commentaries on Wordsworth's self-revisions.

Biography: start with Stephen Gill, *William Wordsworth: A Life* (Oxford: Clarendon Press, 1989); John Williams, *William Wordsworth: A Literary Life* (Basingstoke: Macmillan, 1996); and Juliet Barker, *Wordsworth: A Life* (London: Viking, 2000) and *Wordsworth: A Life in Letters* (London: Viking, 2002). The letters of Wordsworth, Mary, Dorothy and Henry Crabb Robinson are available as a Past Masters electronic resource (InteLex, 2002); for John Wordsworth's correspondence, see Carl H. Ketcham, ed., *The Letters of John Wordsworth* (Ithaca, NY: Cornell University Press, 1969). William Knight, *The Life of William Wordsworth*, 3 vols. (Edinburgh: William Patterson, 1889), Frances Blanshard, *Portraits of Wordsworth* (London: Allen and Unwin, 1959) and Mary Moorman, *William Wordsworth a Biography: The Early Years 1770–1803* and *The Later Years 1803–1850* (Oxford: Clarendon, 1957; 1965) are still helpful. Kenneth R. Johnston, *The Hidden Wordsworth* (London: Pimlico, 2000) caused a stir on first publication, suggesting that Wordsworth may have been a government spy, an assertion deployed in Julian Temple's rather anti-Wordsworth film *Pandaemonium* (2000), and contested by Michael Durey, 'The Spy Who Never Was', *Times Literary Supplement*, 10 March 2000, 14–15. Keith Hanley, *Wordsworth: A Poet's History* (Basingstoke: Palgrave, 2000) and Duncan Wu, *William Wordsworth: An Inner Life* (Oxford: Blackwell, 2002) both use psychoanalysis to address the poet's biography. H. D. Rawnsley, *Reminiscences of Wordsworth among the Peasantry of Westmoreland* (London: Dillon's, 1968) and T. W. Thompson, *Wordsworth's Hawkshead* (Oxford: Oxford University Press, 1970) offer domestic detail. Biographies of Dorothy are also suggestive: start with Frances Wilson, *The Ballad of Dorothy Wordsworth* (London: Faber and Faber, 2008); and then Robert Gittings and Jo Manton, *Dorothy Wordsworth* (Oxford: Oxford University Press, 1985); plus Pamela Woof, *Dorothy Wordsworth: Writer* (Grasmere: Wordsworth Trust, 1988).

Poetics: for an introduction to this topic, see Susan Wolfson, 'Wordsworth's Craft', in Stephen Gill, ed., *The Cambridge Companion to Wordsworth* (Cambridge: Cambridge University Press, 2003), pp.108–24; and Stuart Curran, 'Wordsworth and the Forms of Poetry', in Kenneth R. Johnston and Gene W.

Ruoff, eds., *The Age of William Wordsworth: Critical Essays on the Romantic Tradition* (New Brunswick: Rutgers University Press, 1987), pp.121–6; readers new to prosody might start with a general introduction to the field, such as Rhian Williams, *The Poetry Toolkit: The Essential Guide to Studying Poetry* (London: Continuum, 2009). For detailed studies of Wordsworth's lexicon, see Brennan O'Donnell's *The Passion of Metre: A Study of Wordsworth's Metrical Art* (London: Kent State University Press, 1995); Susan Eilenberg, *Strange Power of Speech: Wordsworth, Coleridge and Literary Possession* (Oxford: Oxford University Press, 1992); and Hugh Sykes Davies, *Wordsworth and the Worth of Words* (Cambridge: Cambridge University Press, 1986). For a theoretical approach, see J. Hillis Miller, 'The Stone and the Shell: The Problem of Poetic Form in Wordsworth's Dream of the Arab', in Robert Ellrodt, ed., *Mouvements premiers: Etudes critiques offertes à Georges Poulet* (Paris: José Corti, 1972), pp.125–47; Paul de Man, *The Rhetoric of Romanticism* (New York: Columbia University Press, 1984); Andrzej Warminski and Cynthia Chase, 'Wordsworth and the Production of Poetry', special issue of *Diacritics*, 17.4 (1987); and Don H. Bialostosky, *Wordsworth, Dialogics, and the Practice of Criticism* (Cambridge: Cambridge University Press, 1992). Stuart Curran, *Poetic Form and British Romanticism* (Oxford: Oxford University Press, 1986) offers a historical account of form, while Olivia Smith, *The Politics of Language, 1798–1819* (Oxford: Clarendon Press, 1984) provides a political one. Christopher Ricks, 'A Pure Organic Pleasure from the Lines', *Essays in Criticism*, 21 (1971), 1–32; and Peter Howarth, 'Wordsworth, Free Verse and Exteriority', *The Wordsworth Circle*, 34.1 (2003), 44–8, are both lively accounts of Wordsworth's innovative poetic experiments; and Robert Rehder tracks the impact of such innovation in *Wordsworth and the Beginnings of Modern Poetry* (London: Croom Helm, 1981).

Major poems: included here are several model analyses, which offer an introduction to both specific texts and examples of how to critically approach individual poems: Jonathan Wordsworth, *The Music of Humanity: A Critical Study of Wordsworth's 'Ruined Cottage'* (London: Nelson, 1969); Stephen Parrish, *The Art of the 'Lyrical Ballads'* (Cambridge, MA: Harvard University Press, 1973); James Butler, 'Wordsworth's *Tuft of Primroses*: "An Unrelenting Doom"', *Studies in Romanticism*, 14.3 (1975), 237–48; W. J. B. Owen, '*The Borderers* and the Aesthetics of Drama', *The Wordsworth Circle*, 6.4 (1975), 227–39; Peter Larkin, 'Wordsworth's "After-Sojourn": Revision and Unself-Rivalry in the Later Poetry', *Studies in Romanticism*, 20.4 (1981), 409–36; Kenneth Johnston, *Wordsworth and 'The Recluse'* (New Haven: Yale University Press, 1984); Judith W. Page, ' "A History / Homely and Rude": Genre and Style in Wordsworth's "Michael" ', *Studies in English Literature*, 29.4 (1989), 621–36; Charles Rzepka,

'A Gift that Complicates Employ: Poetry and Poverty in "Resolution and Independence"', *Studies in Romanticism*, 28.2 (1989), 225–47; Anne Janowitz, ' "A Night on Salisbury Plain": A Dreadful, Ruined Nature', in Keith Hanley and Raman Selden, eds., *Revolution and English Romanticism: Politics and Rhetoric* (London: Harvester Wheatsheaf, 1990), pp.225–40; Stephen Gill, *William Wordsworth: 'The Prelude'* (Cambridge: Cambridge University Press, 1991); Anne L. Rylestone, *Prophetic Memory in Wordsworth's Ecclesiastical Sketches* (Carbondale: Southern Illinois University Press, 1991); Peter J. Manning, 'Troubling the Borders: *Lyrical Ballads* 1798 and 1998', *The Wordsworth Circle*, 30 (1999), 22–6; and Richard Gravil, ' "Tintern Abbey" and *The System of Nature*', *Romanticism*, 6 (2000), 35–54.

Philosophy and religion: before historicism came to dominate literary studies, the question of how to interpret Wordsworth tended towards the philosophical and phenomenological. Geoffrey Hartman's readings of Wordsworth remain, I think, the most important and influential in any field of criticism on the poet, and both *Wordsworth's Poetry 1787–1814* (New Haven: Yale University Press, 1964) and *The Unremarkable Wordsworth* (London: Methuen, 1987) are required and illuminating reading. See also G. Wilson Knight, 'The Wordsworthian Profundity', *The Starlit Dome: Studies in the Poetry of Vision* (London: Oxford University Press, 1941), pp.1–82; John Jones, *The Egotistical Sublime: A History of Wordsworth's Imagination* (Westport, CT: Greenwood Press, 1954); David Ferry, *The Limits of Mortality: An Essay on Wordsworth's Major Poems* (Middletown, CT: Wesleyan University Press, 1959); M. H. Abrams, *Natural Supernaturalism: Tradition and Revolution in Romantic Literature* (New York: Norton, 1971); Thomas Weiskel, *The Romantic Sublime: Studies in the Structure and Psychology of Transcendence* (Baltimore: Johns Hopkins University Press, 1976); Frances Ferguson, *Wordsworth: Language as Counter-Spirit* (New Haven: Yale University Press, 1977); Cynthia Chase, *Decomposing Figures: Rhetorical Readings in the Romantic Tradition* (Baltimore: Johns Hopkins University Press, 1986); David Bromwich, *Disowned by Memory: Wordsworth's Poetry of the 1790s* (Chicago: University of Chicago Press, 1998); Simon Jarvis, 'Wordsworth and Idolatry', *Studies in Romanticism*, 38.1 (1999), 3–27; Richard Eldridge, *The Persistence of Romanticism: Essays in Philosophy and Literature* (Cambridge: Cambridge University Press, 2001); Scott R. Stroud, 'John Dewey and the Question of Artful Communication', *Philosophy and Rhetoric*, 41.2 (2008), 153–83. On religion, see Stephen Prickett, *Romanticism and Religion: The Tradition of Coleridge and Wordsworth in the Victorian Church* (Cambridge: Cambridge University Press, 1976); David P. Haney, *William Wordsworth and the Hermeneutics of Incarnation* (University Park: Pennsylvania State University Press, 1993); John G. Rudy, *Wordsworth and the Zen Mind: The Poetry of Self-emptying* (Albany: State University of New York Press, 1996); Robert Ryan, *The Romantic Reformation: Religious Politics in English Literature 1789–1824* (Cambridge: Cambridge University Press, 1997); Morton Paley, *Apocalypse and Millennium in English Romantic Poetry* (Oxford: Clarendon Press, 1999); David Jasper, *The Sacred and Secular Canon in Romanticism: Preserving the Sacred Truths* (Basingstoke: Macmillan, 1999); Mark Canuel, *Religion, Toleration, and British Writing 1790–1830* (Cambridge: Cambridge University Press, 2002); Daniel E. White, *Early Romanticism and Religious Dissent* (Cambridge: Cambridge University Press, 2006); Colin Jager, *The Book of God: Secularization and Design in the Romantic Era* (Philadelphia: University of Pennsylvania Press, 2007); and Jonathan Roberts, *Blake. Wordsworth. Religion* (London: Continuum, 2010).

Psychoanalysis and gender: given the focus on self-analysis in Wordsworth's poetry, psychoanalytic criticism is an especially apt way into his work. Start with G. Kim Blank, *Wordsworth and Feeling: The Poetry of an Adult Child* (London: Associated University Presses, 1995); and then Richard J. Onorato, *The Character of the Poet: Wordsworth in 'The Prelude'* (Princeton: Princeton University Press, 1971); David Ellis, *Wordsworth, Freud and the Spots of Time: Interpretation in 'The Prelude'* (Cambridge: Cambridge University Press, 1985); Mark Edmundson, *Towards Reading Freud: Self-creation in Milton, Wordsworth, Emerson and Sigmund Freud* (Princeton: Princeton University Press, 1990); W. Speed Hill, 'The Psychic Link', *Textual Cultures: Texts, Contexts, Interpretation*, 3.1 (2008), 56–64; Joel Faflak, *Romantic Psychoanalysis: The Burden of the Mystery* (New York: State University of New York Press, 2008); and Anne-Lise François, *Open Secrets: The Literature of Uncounted Experience* (Stanford: Stanford University Press, 2008). Mary Jacobus's scholarship is a model of how psychoanalysis has focused criticism on questions of gender and sexual difference, see, for example, *Romanticism, Writing, and Sexual Difference: Essays on 'The Prelude'* (Oxford: Clarendon Press, 1989); and see Adela Pinch, 'Female Chatter: Meter, Masochism and the *Lyrical Ballads*', *English Literary History*, 55:4 (1988), 835–52. On Wordsworth's relationship to women and the domestic: start with Anne K. Mellor, ed., *Romanticism and Feminism* (Bloomington: Indiana University Press, 1988), especially Susan J. Wolfson's essay 'Individual in Community: Dorothy Wordsworth in Conversation with William', pp.139–66; and then Marlon B. Ross 'Naturalizing Gender: Woman's Place in Wordsworth's Ideological Landscape', *English Literary History*, 53:2 (1986), 391–410; Gayatri Chakravorty Spivak, 'Sex and History in *The Prelude* (1805): Books IX to XIII', in Richard Machin and Christopher Norris, eds., *Post-structuralist Readings of English Poetry* (Cambridge: Cambridge University Press, 1987), pp.193–226; Theresa M. Kelley, *Wordsworth's Revisionary*

Aesthetics (Cambridge: Cambridge University Press, 1988); Judith Page, *Wordsworth and the Cultivation of Women* (Berkeley: University of California Press, 1994); Anne K. Mellor, 'A Criticism of Their Own: Romantic Women Literary Critics', in John Beer, ed., *Questioning Romanticism* (Baltimore: Johns Hopkins University Press, 1995), pp.29–48; Elizabeth A. Fay, *Becoming Wordsworthian: A Performative Aesthetics* (Amherst: University of Massachusetts Press, 1995); John Barrell, '"Laodamia" and the Moaning of Mary', *Textual Practice*, 10.3 (1996), 449–77; John Powell Ward, '"Will No One Tell Me What She Sings?": Women and Gender in the Poetry of William Wordsworth', *Studies in Romanticism*, 36.4 (1997), 611–33; and Heidi Thomson, '"We Are Two": The Address to Dorothy in "Tintern Abbey"', *Studies in Romanticism*, 40 (2001), 531–46.

Politics and historicism: the material rather than transcendental conditions of Wordsworth's work came into focus in the 1970s: see E. P. Thompson, 'Disenchantment or Default? A Lay Sermon', in Conor Cruise O'Brien and W. D. Vanech, eds., *Power and Consciousness* (London: University of London Press, 1969), pp.149–81; Carl Woodring, *Politics in English Romantic Poetry* (Cambridge, MA: Harvard University Press, 1970); Leslie F. Chard, *Dissenting Republican: Wordsworth's Early Life and Thought in Their Political Context* (The Hague: Mouton, 1972); and Michael Friedman, *The Making of a Tory Humanist: William Wordsworth and the Idea of Community* (New York: Columbia University Press, 1979). New historicism followed, intent on positioning Wordsworth as a reactionary, rather than radical figure: James Chandler labels him a Burkean in *Wordsworth's Second Nature: A Study of the Poetry and the Politics* (Chicago: University of Chicago Press, 1984); and see also Marilyn Butler, *Romantics, Rebels and Reactionaries* (Oxford: Oxford University Press, 1982); Jerome McGann, *The Romantic Ideology: A Critical Investigation* (Chicago: University of Chicago Press, 1983); Marjorie Levinson, *Wordsworth's Great Period Poems* (Cambridge: Cambridge University Press, 1986); David Simpson, *Wordsworth's Historical Imagination: The Poetry of Displacement* (London: Methuen, 1987); Alan Liu, *Wordsworth: The Sense of History* (Stanford: Stanford University Press, 1988); and Clifford Siskin, 'Working *The Prelude*: Foucault and the New History', in Nigel Wood, ed., *The Prelude* (Buckingham: Open University Press, 1993), all studies that accuse him of displacing political ideas from his works. For a less subjective and more detailed response to Wordsworth's politics, see Nicholas Roe, *Wordsworth and Coleridge: The Radical Years* (Oxford: Clarendon Press, 1988); and for a response to new historical criticism see Helen Vendler, '"Tintern Abbey": Two Assaults', *Bucknell Review*, 36.1 (1992), 173–90; and Thomas McFarland, *William Wordsworth: Intensity and Achievement* (Oxford: Clarendon Press,

1992). On Wordsworth's revolutionary politics, see Kenneth R. Johnston, 'Philanthropy or Treason? Wordsworth as "Active Partisan"', *Studies in Romanticism*, 25.3 (1986), 371–409; John Williams, *Wordsworth: Romantic Poetry and Revolution Politics* (Manchester: Manchester University Press, 1989); Richard Bourke, *Romantic Discourse and Political Modernity: Wordsworth, the Intellectual and Cultural Critique* (London: Harvester Wheatsheaf, 1993); and Gregory Dart, *Robespierre, Rousseau and English Romanticism* (Cambridge: Cambridge University Press, 1999). On economics in Wordsworth, see Gary Harrison, *Wordsworth's Vagrant Muse: Poetry, Poverty and Power* (Detroit: Wayne State University Press, 1994); David Chandler, 'Wordsworth versus Malthus: The Political Context of "The Old Cumberland Beggar"', *Charles Lamb Bulletin*, 115 (2001), 72–85; Philip Connell, *Romanticism, Economics, and the Question of 'Culture'* (Oxford: Oxford University Press, 2001); Tom Duggett, 'Celtic Night and Gothic Grandeur: Politics and Antiquarianism in Wordsworth's "Salisbury Plain"', *Romanticism*, 13.2 (2007), 164–76; and James M. Garrett, *Wordsworth and the Writing of the Nation* (Aldershot: Ashgate, 2008).

Eco- and ethical criticism: Jonathan Bate, *Romantic Ecology: Wordsworth and the Environmental Tradition* (London: Routledge, 1991) and *The Song of the Earth* (London: Picador, 2001) remain influential; and see also Karl Kroeber, '"Home at Grasmere": Ecological Holiness', *PMLA*, 89.1 (1974), 132–41 and *Ecological Literary Criticism: Romantic Imagining and the Biology of Mind* (New York: Columbia University Press, 1994); plus Donald Hayden, 'William Wordsworth: Early Ecologist', in T. M. Hanwell, ed., *Studies in Relevance: Romantic and Victorian Writers in 1972* (Salzburg: University of Salzburg, 1973), pp.36–52. Other useful sources include Ralph Pite, 'How Green Were the Romantics', *Studies in Romanticism*, 35.3 (1996), 357–74; James C. McKusick, 'Introduction' to a special issue on 'Romanticism and Ecology', *The Wordsworth Circle*, 28.3 (1997), 123–4; Heather Frey, 'Defining the Self, Defiling the Countryside: Travel Writing and Romantic Ecology', *The Wordsworth Circle*, 28.3 (1997), 162–6; Kevin Hutchings, 'Ecocriticism in British Romantic Studies', *Literature Compass*, 4.1 (2007), 172–202; and Kenneth R. Cervelli, *Dorothy Wordsworth's Ecology* (London: Routledge, 2007). On Wordsworth's relationship to the landscape, see: Peter Bicknell and Robert Woof, *The Discovery of the Lake District 1750–1810: A Context for Wordsworth* (Grasmere: Trustees of Dove Cottage, 1982); Mary R. Wedd, 'Light on Landscape in Wordsworth's "Spots of Time"', *The Wordsworth Circle*, 14:4 (1983), 224–32; Matthew Brennan, *Wordsworth, Turner, and Romantic Landscape: A Study in the Traditions of the Picturesque and the Sublime* (Columbia, SC: Camden House, 1987); Anne Janowitz, *England's Ruins: Poetic Purpose and the National Landscape* (Oxford: Blackwell, 1990); John Wyatt,

Wordsworth and the Geologists (Cambridge: Cambridge University Press, 1995); Celeste Langan, *Romantic Vagrancy: Wordsworth and the Simulation of Freedom* (Cambridge: Cambridge University Press, 1995); Tim Fulford, *Landscape, Liberty and Authority: Poetry, Criticism and Politics from Thomson to Wordsworth* (Basingstoke: Macmillan, 1996); Jonathan Bate, 'Living with the Weather', *Studies in Romanticism*, 35.3 (1996), 431–48; Robin Jarvis, *Romantic Writing and Pedestrian Travel* (Basingstoke: Macmillan, 1997); and Michael Wiley, *Romantic Geography: Wordsworth and Anglo-European Spaces* (Basingstoke: Macmillan, 1998); Toby Benis, *Romanticism on the Road: The Marginal Gains of Wordsworth's Homeless* (Basingstoke: Macmillan, 2000); and Nicholas Roe, *The Politics of Nature: William Wordsworth and Some Contemporaries* (Basingstoke: Palgrave, 2002). On ethical criticism, see Wayne C. Booth, *The Company We Keep: An Ethics of Fiction* (Berkeley: University of California Press, 1988); Martha C. Nussbaum, *Poetic Justice: Literary Imagination and Public Life* (Boston, MA: Beacon Press, 1995); Todd F. Davis and Kenneth Womack, eds., *Mapping the Ethical Turn: A Reader in Ethics, Culture and Literary Theory* (Charlottesville: University Press of Virginia, 2001), and R. Clifton Spargo, *The Ethics of Mourning: Grief and Responsibility in Elegiac Literature* (Baltimore: Johns Hopkins University Press, 2004).

Reception and influence: begin with the anecdotal but illuminating Edith J. Morley, ed., *Henry Crabb Robinson on Books and Their Writers*, 3 vols. (London: J. M. Dent, 1938) and scholarly Stephen Gill, *Wordsworth and the Victorians* (Oxford: Clarendon Press, 1998). On Wordsworth's contemporary reception, see John O. Hayden, *The Romantic Reviewers 1802–1824* (1969) and *Romantic Bards and British Reviewers* (London: Routledge and Kegan Paul, 1971); and Donald Reiman, *The Romantics Reviewed: Contemporary Reviews of British Romantic Writers* (New York: Garland, 1972). Robert Woof, *William Wordsworth: The Critical Heritage* (London: Routledge, 2001) is a useful collection of sources; and Katherine M. Peek, *Wordsworth in England: Studies in the History of His Fame* (New York: Octagon, 1969) and Joel Pace and Matthew Scott, *Wordsworth in American Literary Culture* (Basingstoke: Macmillan, 2005) locate Wordsworth in different national traditions. Commentaries on parodies of the poet include Nicola Trott, 'Wordsworth in the Nursery: The Parodic School of Criticism', *The Wordsworth Circle*, 32 (2001), 66–77; and John Strachan's special issue of *Romanticism on the Net*, 'Romantic Parody', 15 (1999). On literary influence, see Jonathan Bate, *Shakespeare and the English Romantic Imagination* (Oxford: Clarendon Press, 1986); Robin Jarvis, *Wordsworth, Milton and the Theory of Poetic Relations* (Basingstoke: Macmillan, 1991); Lucy Newlyn, *'Paradise Lost' and the Romantic Reader* (Oxford: Clarendon Press, 1993); Robert J. Griffin, *Wordsworth's Pope: A Study of Literary Historiography* (Cambridge: Cambridge University Press, 1995); and Claudia Moscovici, *Romanticism and Postromanticism* (Lanham: Lexington, 2007). On Wordsworth's influence, see Kenneth Johnston, 'Wordsworth, Frost, Stevens and the Poetic Vocation', *Studies in Romanticism*, 21.1 (1982), 87–100; D. D. Devlin, *De Quincey, Wordsworth and the Art of Prose* (London: Macmillan, 1983); Heather Glen, *Vision and Disenchantment: Blake's 'Songs' and Wordsworth's 'Lyrical Ballads'* (Cambridge: Cambridge University Press, 1983); Jack Stillinger, 'Wordsworth and Keats', in Johnston and Ruoff, eds., *Age of William Wordsworth*, pp. 173–95; Annabel Patterson, 'Hard Pastoral: Frost, Wordsworth, and Modernist Poetics', *Criticism*, 29.1 (1987), 67–87; G. Kim Blank, *Wordsworth's Influence on Shelley: A Study of Poetic Authority* (London: Macmillan, 1988); Laura Quinney, *The Poetics of Disappointment: Wordsworth to Ashbery* (Charlottesville: University Press of Virginia, 1999); Anne Ferry, 'Revisions of Visions: Wordsworth and his Inheritors', *Raritan*, 21 (2001), 67–93; Michael O'Neill, ' "O Shining in Modest Glory": Contemporary Northern Irish Poets and Romantic Poetry', *The Wordsworth Circle*, 32 (2001), 59–65; Richard Cronin, *Romantic Victorians: English Literature 1824–1840* (Basingstoke: Palgrave, 2002); and Damian Walford Davies and Richard Marggraf Turley, eds., *The Monstrous Debt: Modalities of Romantic Influence in Twentieth-century Literature* (Detroit: Wayne State University Press, 2006). The reciprocal influence between Wordsworth and Coleridge is widely commented on: see Thomas McFarland, *Romanticism and the Forms of Ruin: Wordsworth, Coleridge and Modalities of Fragmentation* (Princeton: Princeton University Press, 1981); Lucy Newlyn, *Coleridge, Wordsworth and the Language of Allusion* (Oxford: Clarendon Press, 1986); Gene Ruoff, *Wordsworth and Coleridge: The Making of the Major Lyrics, 1802–1904* (London: Harvester Wheatsheaf, 1989); and Adam Sisman, *The Friendship: Wordsworth and Coleridge* (London: HarperPress, 2006).

Reference: there is an abundance of bibliographic material on Wordsworth; of primary importance are Wordsworth's own reading practices, documented in Duncan Wu, *Wordsworth's Reading 1770–1799* and *Wordsworth's Reading 1800–1815* (Cambridge: Cambridge University Press, 1993; 1995); and Chester L. Shaver and Alice C. Shaver, *Wordsworth's Library: A Catalogue* (New York: Garland, 1979). Richard W. Clancey offers a solid overview of his classical reading in *Wordsworth's Classical Undersong: Education, Rhetoric and Poetic Truth* (Basingstoke: Macmillan, 2000). Lane Cooper's *A Concordance to the Poems of William Wordsworth* (London: Smith, Elder, 1911) offers a different reading experience to online versions. For records of Wordsworthian criticism, start with Nicholas Roe, 'William Wordsworth', in Michael O'Neill, ed., *Literature of the Romantic Period: A Bibliographical Guide* (Oxford: Oxford

University Press, 1998), pp.45–64; and Keith Hanley and David Barron, *An Annotated Critical Bibliography of William Wordsworth* (London: Prentice Hall, 1995). Further detail is available in Stephen N. Bauer, *William Wordsworth, A Reference Guide to British Criticism, 1793–1899* (Boston, MA: G. K. Hall, 1978); Elton F. Henley and David H. Stam, *Wordsworthian Criticism 1945–64: An Annotated Bibliography* (New York: New York Public Library, 1965); David H. Stam, *Wordsworthian Criticism 1964–73: An Annotated Bibliography* (New York: New York Public Library, 1974); and Mark Jones and Karl Kroeber, *Wordsworth Scholarship and Criticism, 1973–1984: An Annotated Bibliography, with Selected Criticism, 1809–1972* (New York: Garland, 1985). Finally, Mark L. Reed's research on Wordsworth's complete writing is available in *Wordsworth: The Chronology of the Early Years, 1770–1799* (Cambridge, MA: Harvard University Press, 1967) and *Wordsworth: The Chronology of the Middle Years* (Cambridge, MA: Harvard University Press, 1975).

Index

Cambridge Introductions to...

AUTHORS

TOPICS

Printed in the United States
By Bookmasters